The Business of Human Services

A Guide to Running a Successful Human Services Company

CASE STUDY WORKBOOK

by James G. Balestrieri *with* Terrence J. Leahy

The Business of Human Services:
A Guide to Running a Successful Human Services Company:
Case Study Workbook

Writers of the Round Table Press
PO Box 511
Highland Park, IL 60035
www.roundtablecompanies.com

RTC Publishing is an imprint of Writers of the Round Table, Inc. Writers of the Round Table Press and the RTC Publishing logo are trademarks of Writers of the Round Table, Inc.

Illustration: *Nathan Lueth*
Publisher: *Corey Michael Blake*
Post Production: *David Charles Cohen*
Directoress of Happiness: *Erin Cohen*
Director of Author Services: *Kristin Westberg*
Facts Keeper: *Mike Winicour*
Original Front Cover Design: *Analee Paz*
Cover Modification, Back Cover: *Sunny DiMartino*
Interior Design and Layout: *Sunny DiMartino*
Proofreading: *Rita Hess*
Last Looks: *Sunny DiMartino*
Indexing: *Linda Presto*
Digital Book Conversion: *Sunny DiMartino*
Digital Publishing: *Sunny DiMartino*

Printed in the United States of America
First Edition: May 2013
10 9 8 7 6 5 4 3 2

Library of Congress Cataloging-in-Publication Data
Balestrieri, James G.
The Business of human services: a guide to running a successful human services company: case study workbook / James G. Balestrieri, Terrence J. Leahy.— 1st ed. p. cm.
Print ISBN: 978-1-939418-31-9
Digital ISBN: 978-1-939418-30-2
Library of Congress Control Number: 2013938906

CONTENTS

PREFACE

This case study book serves as a companion to the text *The Business of Human Services: A Guide to Running a Successful Human Services Company*. A more complete understanding of our industry requires not only studying the text chapters, but also applying those principles to situations that have occurred in real life. Reality is a wicked teacher. In our day-to-day work, we face opportunities to make decisions that can lead to nirvana or to disaster. Whether we confront a situation involving conflicting rules, government agencies working at cross purposes, or cloudy strategic direction, there is no shortage of challenges.

It is our hope that you can use the text and case study book together to help you achieve your mission. Whether the answers are in black and white or reside in the cloudier world of grey, your studies will place you and your agency on the right path so you can control your own destiny.

You may notice that certain words or phrases are placed in quotes. This is intended to emphasize key teachings, concepts, and ideas. I hope this is not overdone.

Good decisions really do make a difference! The landscape is littered with human services companies that had noble missions but stumbled along the way, either failing to achieve their full potential or disappearing altogether. Our industry is special, and like any specialized industry, it demands specialized ways to make effective decisions. Let us help you fill your toolbox with the tools necessary for success. Good luck, and thank you for undertaking this important journey.

James G. Balestrieri
President/CEO
Oconomowoc Residential Programs

AMERICAN SENIOR LIVING CENTERS (ASLC)

Case Overview

ASLC was a human services company that was a subsidiary of the Oconomowoc Residential Programs, Inc. (ORP) specializing in providing various types of assisted living options for elderly adults. Its first program opened in 1988, and it was sold in late spring 1998 to a nursing home operator for reasons that will be explored later in the case. At its peak in the mid-1990s, it operated six 20-bed community-based residential facilities (CBRFs), one 20-bed CBRF for individuals afflicted with Alzheimer's disease (or other dementia), and one residential care apartment complex (RCAC) consisting of 44 apartments, with a capacity of approximately 200 individuals and one more facility under development at the time of sale.

The 1990s was a time of explosive growth in the arena of elderly services. Hospital chains, real estate developers, and business entrepreneurs were among those trying to enter this market space. The buzz around the business opportunities triggered by the major demographic movement of the "aging of America" triggered the growth.

ASLC began from scratch but was a member of a family of human services companies providing similar services, with which it shared many of its systems, policies, procedures, philosophies, and staff.

The operations were situated throughout the Milwaukee, Wisconsin, metro area. Community supports for the clients, ranging from medical to recreational to family, were nearby. The company was near the parent company, which could provide shared support services such as group purchasing and building maintenance that helped the bottom line.

First, let's review pertinent parts of a 1997 "Opinion of Value" prepared for ASLC's parent company, ORP, Inc. This will get us up to speed on the company, the industry, and the environment present in the mid-1990s.

Second, we will take a journey through *The Business of Human Services*, using certain chapters to apply the lessons and concepts to the ASLC case. We will explore the thinking that led to the decision to sell ASLC and seek your opinion on whether they did the right thing for ORP.

Background Information

The Services. ORP operated an array of human service programs for people with disabilities in the 1990s. The senior living facilities were operated through ORP's ASLC division.

The ASLC programs offered a high level of personal care, staffed with resident care specialists, 24 hours per day. Nutritious meals and snacks were planned and professionally prepared on the premises. An on-site staff nurse provided health and medication monitoring. Recreation and leisure time activities and outings occurred daily. Each facility provided transportation with its own vehicles. Housekeeping and maintenance were offered, along with personal laundry assistance. There was a 24-hour emergency response team, and all entrances were monitored by alarms. ASLC offered Alzheimer and dementia care in one of the CBRF units. These services helped support "aging in place."

The Facilities. The ASLC operations consisted of nine residential properties located in southeastern Wisconsin. Seven of these properties were state licensed as CBRFs. They were located in the Milwaukee metropolitan area close to shopping, churches, parks, and medical facilities. Each CBRF resident had a private room with a private or semi-private bathroom. While considered adequate at the time of renovation, the semi-private bathrooms were generally not being developed any more in the late 1990s.

The two assisted living facilities that opened later in the ASLC evolution were built previously and needed adaptations to fit market needs. Living units ranged from private studios to two-bedroom apartments, all with private baths. They also included wellness/fitness centers, beauty/barber shops, general stores, hobby and craft rooms, private dining rooms, pet wings, on-site banking, and other specialized services.

The facilities were either newer or renovated within 10 years of the sale date. Adequate parking was provided through either surface lots or street parking.

1. Marjorie C. Home, Wauwatosa, Wisconsin. This elevator-equipped home was licensed as a 20-bed, Class B CBRF. The facility was renovated in September 1991. The occupancy on the date of sale was 95%, with average rent per unit of $24,924. The average adjusted expense per unit was $19,591. The building showed no signs of deferred maintenance.

2. Wabash Home, Milwaukee, Wisconsin. This elevator-equipped facility was licensed as a 20-bed, Class B CBRF. Renovation work was completed in September 1989. Occupancy on the date of sale was 90%, with an average rent per unit of $22,824 per year. Average adjusted expense per unit was $18,613. The building showed no signs of deferred maintenance.

3. Fardale Home, Milwaukee, Wisconsin. The facility was licensed as a 20-bed, Class B CBRF. Renovation work was completed in the early 1990s. The occupancy on the date of sale was 100%, with an average rent per unit of $23,724 per year. Average adjusted expense per unit was $18,285. The building showed no signs of deferred maintenance.

4. Grantosa Home, Milwaukee, Wisconsin. This elevator-equipped facility was licensed as a 20-bed, Class B CBRF. Renovation work was completed in September 1992. The occupancy on the date of sale was 100%, with an average rent per unit of $24,720 per year. Average adjusted expense per unit was $18,676. The building showed no signs of deferred maintenance.

5. Sunnyridge Home, Wisconsin. This elevator-equipped facility was licensed as a 20-bed, Class B CBRF. The facility housed 16 living units, and 4 units were used as office space. This space could be converted back to units if needed. Renovation work was completed in August 1993. Occupancy on the date of sale was 75% (15 beds), with average rent per unit of $24,612 per year. The average adjusted expense per unit was $21,082. The building showed no signs of deferred maintenance.

6. Marian Heights, Port Washington, Wisconsin. This 17-bed elevator-equipped facility was a Class B CBRF. Renovation work was completed in May 1994. The occupancy on the date of sale was 95%, with an average rent per unit of $24,816 per year. Average adjusted expense per unit was $19,903. The building showed no signs of deferred maintenance. This home was leased from St. Mary's Congregation, Inc., with an annual lease of $42,230 for fiscal 1997. The lease was triple net with an initial term of six years commencing in October 1993. Two four-year renewal options required nine months' prior notice. Rent was adjusted annually by the percentage change in the Consumer Price Index. The lease was based on the number of beds the facility was licensed to operate.

7. Michele Home, Milwaukee, Wisconsin. This elevator-equipped facility was licensed as a 20-bed, Class B CBRF. Renovation work was completed in September 1989 and again in December 1996. As a result, the building was still in a lease-up stage, building up to the date of sale. Occupancy was 75%, with average rent per unit of $28,980. Average adjusted expense per unit was $21,110. This facility provided Alzheimer and dementia care. The building showed no signs of deferred maintenance but was located in an area that was showing signs of economic stress.

8. Kingswood Place, Fond du Lac, Wisconsin. Construction of this new 30-bed assisted and independent living facility was substantially completed in August 1997, with lease-up commencing September 1997. The occupancy was 0% at the date of sale. The pro forma average rent per unit for 30 units was estimated at $21,966, and the average adjusted expense per unit was estimated at $23,343. In October 1996, an entity related to ORP entered into a lease agreement with a developer to take over a partially completed senior apartment complex. This lease was for a 20-year term with base annual rents of $233,640 per year. ORP had an option to purchase the property at fair market value after three years. The owner had indicated that subsequent to exercising the purchase option, the property would quality for HUD financing, with an interest rate of 8.25% and 25-year amortization (very favorable for that time).

In addition, the landlord was entitled to additional rent equal to 15% of ORP's net operating income prior to management fees. Other costs that could have been incurred but that were not obligations under the lease included financing for furniture and equipment and the lease-up deficit. These capital costs were estimated at $90,000 and $55,000, respectively, on the date of sale.

9. Wilkinson Woods, Oconomowoc, Wisconsin. Renovation work on this 40-bed assisted and independent living facility was completed in late 1996 with lease-up commencing in 1997. This elevator-equipped unit had an occupancy level of 85% with an average rent per unit of $14,796 and an adjusted average expense per unit of $18,181. The building showed no signs of deferred maintenance and was very attractive.

The Industry Overview. An assisted living residence combines housing, personal care services, supervision, and healthcare in a home-like atmosphere. Supply and demand for assisted living residences have flourished as a welcome alternative to nursing homes for many elderly people who can no longer care for themselves due to physical or cognitive frailties but who do not need skilled medical care. More and more Americans are choosing this compassionate and less costly alternative for themselves and for their family members in need of long-term care. Typically, such residents require assistance in one or more activities of daily living (ADLs), including housework, shopping, and meal preparation, as well as some level of personal care. Residences are typically in the middle of continuum of care, between independent living and a skilled nursing facility (SNF). Some assisted living facilities are specialized to serve unique health care markets such as Alzheimer's disease patients.

The Demand for Services. The market for assisted living services at the time of sale was larger than most people realized and was continuing to grow. For example, according to the U.S. Census Bureau, there were approximately 3.5 million people age 85, or older, and that number was projected to increased 42% during the 1990s and 31% from 2000 and 2010. The increase was largely driven by the baby boom and major increases in life expectancy due to medical advances. According to the U.S. General Accounting Office, approximately 7 million older people needed assistance with ADLs in the mid-1990s, a figure projected to double by the year 2020.

According to a 1990s study in *Assisted Living Today*, assisted living is an economically attractive alternative to both home health and SNFs because of favorable costs (see table).

Service/Expense	Assisted Living	Home Health	Nursing
Basic monthly cost	$2,250	$3,894	$4,276
Insurance, taxes, etc.	N/A	$527	N/A
Total cost (monthly)	$2,250	$4,421	$4,276

Costs based on average for three states: MI, PA, and NY
Source: Jo Ann Clipp, "Pursuing the Frail Elderly" in Assisted Living Today

Some states provided subsidies in the form of Medicaid Waiver programs or Supplemental Security Income payments, which helped cover the daily rate costs for individuals seeking services, but usually families paid for assisted living services out of their own financial resources, as few seniors had long-term care insurance.

The real estate projects associated with this type of care were many and diverse. The more common ones were: residential care facilities, residential care facilities for the elderly, community-based residential facilities (CBRFs), personal care facilities, assisted living facilities (ALFs), residential care homes, board and care facilities, senior hotels, adult homes, domiciliary facilities, retirement homes, and community residences.

Facilities ranged in size and service offerings. Typical facilities housed between 25 and 125 individuals; however, some projects could range as high as 250 beds. The trend at the time had been to build larger facilities, with many of the older facilities consisting of converted single family or multi-family homes.

The assisted living industry was highly fragmented and characterized by numerous small operators in the 1990s. The scope of services varied substantially from one operator to another, and few provided a comprehensive range of care, such as that needed by those suffering from Alzheimer's. Many advocacy groups were emphasizing the advantages of an ALF over an SNF in terms of quality of life issues for the elderly, very similar to the messaging heard for those with disabilities. In addition, ALFs were targeting what many thought was a very lucrative private pay market. The industry was also experiencing strong growth, as well as rapid consolidation in the 1990s, similar to that experienced in the nursing home industry.

The Supply of Services. According to *Retirement Housing Options: A Resource Manual for the Community, Patients and Families of the MCW Senior Health Program at Froedtert Hospital* in Milwaukee, there were at least 117 independent and assisted living facilities in Wisconsin in the mid-1990s. Some assisted living options for seniors were not actually licensed or highly regulated by the State of Wisconsin; however, the state did set standards to determine whether a facility was eligible to receive various types of medical assistance funding. The average monthly rent in Wisconsin for assisted living and independent living was $1,300, and the average facility age was five years old.

As far as CBRFs in the state, according to the State of Wisconsin Office of Regulations and Licensing, metropolitan Milwaukee was home to over 3,900 elderly CBRF beds in June of 1996. CBRFs are state-licensed and state-regulated facilities.

County	Number of CBRFs	Number of Beds
Milwaukee	84	2,198
Waukesha	43	1,144
Washington	16	350
Ozaukee	14	243
Total	157	3,935

The average monthly rent for Wisconsin CBRFs, as reported in *Retirement Housing Options*, was between $1,700 and $2,000, with an average facility age of 12 years. The following tables compare the capacity and monthly rate of ORP's CBRF properties to others in the marketplace.

COMPARABLE CBRFS – RENTAL RANGE FOR MILWAUKEE/WAUKESHA METRO AREA

Facility Name	Capacity	Monthly Rate
A Loving Home, Inc.	8	$2,200–$2,500
Alternative Living Services	8–60	$2,250–$3,000
**American Senior Living Centers (ASLC) (current average rent/unit: $1,902–$2,405 for the 7 CBRFs)	20	$1,720–$2,700
Bennington Home	6	$1,850–$2,160
Country Range Group	7	$1,400
Cozy Care	7	$2,260–$2,320
Creative Living Environments	8–30	$1,650–$2,700
Fairview Group Homes	8–11	$1,600–$2,400
The B's Our House, Inc.	8	$1,800
Good Manor Hope, Inc.	8	$1,320–$1,520
The Granville Home	8	$1,450–$1,500
Halpin Manor	8	$1,650–$2,250
Hampton House	7	$2,000–$2,200
Home Living Services, Inc.	6–8	$2,100–$2,500
Iris Manor	8	$1,650–$2,200
Rainbow Park Home	6	$1,950
Remember Me Group Home	8	$1,550–$2,450
Seniorminiums	8	$1,768–$2,080
Shoreline Residence, Inc.	20	$1,700–$1,900
Spring Lake	8	$1,150–$1,300
Tall Oaks	20	$1,200–$1,500
Average		$1,725–$2,175

**ASLC Programs

COMPARABLE INDEPENDENT AND ASSISTED LIVING FACILITIES – RENTAL RANGE FOR MILWAUKEE/ WAUKESHA METRO AREA

Facility Name	Monthly Costs
The Arboretum	$920–$1,395
Brookfield Woods	$485–$1,375
The Concord	$1,450–$1,600
Forest Ridge	$795–$875
Harbor Village	$825–$1,120
Hawthorne Terrace	$610–$1,395
Heritage Place	$1,050–$1,175
**Kingswood Place	$1,750–$2,095
Lasata Heights	$620–$923
Laurel Oaks	$900–$2,075
Library Square	$510–$1,055
Linden Ridge	$1,675–$1,975
Muskego Regency	$650–$800
National Regency	$850–$1,100
Pleasantview Apartment	$485–$625
Tamarack Place	$1,175–$1,675
**Wilkinson Woods	$1,160–$2,330
Willowbrook Court	$785–$1,450
Average	$860–$1,290

**ASLC Programs

Sources: ASLC appraisal dated 9/19/1997

Approaches to Value – Income vs. Market (See Chapter 25 in Text)

The Income Approach. The value estimate for CBRFs and assisted living facilities is generally calculated using the "income" approach (the value in use) or the "market" approach (finding comparable sales). In this case, it was difficult to find comparables because the facilities were special purpose properties renovated away from their intended purpose (normal housing), and this special use meant that consideration needed to be given for the more limited use of the property. Because of this, the income approach was used.

The income approach identifies and quantifies revenue sources to estimate gross potential income. Revenue was based on an analysis of historic income, historic occupancy, and current rent roll information. A deduction was then made for an allowance for vacancy, collection, and turnover loss. The effective gross income is the sum of these two items. Historical financial statements are then reviewed to determine operating expenses associated with each property. These departmental expenses were categorized into traditional appraisal categories. This allowed for a comparison of expenses to national and regional averages.

Adjustments were made to both the income and expenses in order to "normalize" these figures. Revenue adjustments were made in the case where the property was in a lease-up phase or rents were significantly below market rates. An adjustment was made to allow for a 6% management fee. In addition, the corporate expense of marketing salaries and the corresponding fringe benefits were deducted from operating expenses because a purchaser is assumed to have corporate infrastructure in place and would not attribute those costs to the properties.

Earnings Before Interest, Taxes, Depreciation, and Amortization (EBITDA). EBITDA, as it was derived for the properties, was equal to adjusted net operating income and was derived from the sum of the effective gross income and the total operating expense. This number was then capitalized to arrive at the property value. The estimate for the appropriate capitalization rate was made from comparable sales of properties, both regionally and nationally. It is the value based on the concept that the buyer will arrange his own financing and the seller discharges its existing debt, if any. The buyer does not assume any of the seller's liabilities other than the continuation of payments on leases. For the properties under consideration, all debt was at market rates. An important side note: Sometimes a property owner holds an assumable below market debt instrument. If this is the case, it will positively affect the value of the property due to the benefit that would accrue to the purchaser.

The Capitalization Rate. A capitalization rate is derived from market factors and can be calculated by dividing a property's cash flow (before taxes and capital costs, and after management fees) by the sale price of the property. The "cap rate" incorporates the cost of debt, as well as the anticipated return on equity.

Influences on variation in cap rates include location, perceived risk, stability of income, age and size of facility, and staffing requirements. Because of the facility age and layout, the Wilkinson Woods and Kingswood projects had a lower cap rate range (10.5–11.5%, which is good) than the CBRFs (12–13%). The CBRFs' lack of attached bathrooms and the small bedroom size (less than 200 square feet) contributed to a higher cap rate range, thereby lowering the ultimate sales value.

The Financials.

1. Valuation summaries: Base year. (See Exhibit #1 for details.)

THE PROPERTIES VALUATION SUMMARY
BASE YEAR[1]

	Cap Rate 12.0%	Cap Rate 13.0%	EIM[3] 1.35
Marjorie C. Home	$932,000	$861,000	$606,000
Wabash Home	$596,000	$550,000	$555,000
Fardale Home	$836,000	$772,000	$576,000
Michele Home	$1,120,000	$1,034,000	$704,000
Sunnyridge Home	$434,000	$404,000	$478,000
Grantosa Home	$889,000	$822,000	$601,000
Marian Heights	$345,000	$318,000	$513,000
Kingswood Place[1,2]	N/A	N/A	$1,076,000
Wilkinson Woods[1]	$2,443,000	$2,274,000	$1,283,000
Total Value	$7,600,000	$7,000,000	$6,400,000
Total Value/Unit	$35,000	$32,000	$29,000

Base year values consider the properties' current year or "as is" value.

1. Cap rates for these properties are 10.5–11.5%.
2. No cap rate used – occupancy zero.
3. An alternate real estate investment analysis measure which measures the effective gross income of a property and adjusts it to market.

2. Valuation summaries: Stabilized year.

THE PROPERTIES VALUATION SUMMARY
STABILIZED YEAR[1]

	Cap Rate 12.0%	Cap Rate 13.0%	EIM[3] 1.35
Marjorie C. Home	$932,000	$861,000	$606,000
Wabash Home	$596,000	$550,000	$555,000
Fardale Home	$836,000	$772,000	$576,000
Michele Home	$1,120,000	$1,034,000	$704,000
Sunnyridge Home	$1,131,000	$1,044,000	$578,000
Grantosa Home	$889,000	$822,000	$601,000
Marian Heights	$345,000	$318,000	$513,000
Kingswood Place[1,2]	N/A	N/A	$1,076,000
Wilkinson Woods[1]	$3,304,000	$3,016,000	$1,283,000
Total Value	$9,200,000	$8,400,000	$6,500,000
Total Value/Unit	$42,000	$38,000	$30,000

Stabilized valuation assumptions are based on the following prospective actions: a) Kingswood Place adds 10 units to the current 30-unit facility, and the units are leased at current market rates; b) Wilkinson Woods turns over its below-market units, and the property is leased to full occupancy; and c) four office units of Sunnyridge are converted back to rentable units and re-leased at market rates.

1. Cap rates for these properties are 10.5–11.5%.
2. No cap rate used – occupancy zero.
3. An alternate real estate investment analysis measure which measures the effective gross income of a property and adjusts it to market.

Comparable Transactions. The following list of recent assisted living facility transactions were used as a basis for deriving the properties' cap rates and EIM.

Location	Beds	Revenue	Net Income	Acquisition Price	Price Per Bed	Price/ Revenue	Cap	Transaction Date

1. Target Name: *Heartland Retirement Services (HRS)*

Terms: $5.5 million in cash; $3.5 million in assumed debt; issuance of 261,424 shares of common stock.

Description: HRS operated 20 facilities for about 350 residents throughout Wisconsin called WovenHearts residences. WovenHearts residences are smaller facilities, with a capacity of 15–26 residences. The company owns 12 units and leases the rest. The average monthly amount paid in March 1996 by residents was $1,560. Occupancy ranged from 31–100%. Heartland also had 14 additional facilities under development at the time of the acquisition, which were expected to be completed in 1996. With full occupancy, the 20 facilities might be able to generate $6.5 million per year, which would yield a price-to-revenue multiplier of 1.34.

Comparison with ORP: Excellent comparable. Comparable unit sizes, rates, and development stage of several facilities makes this the best comparable.

Location	Beds	Revenue	Net Income	Acquisition Price	Price Per Bed	Price/ Revenue	Cap	Transaction Date
Milwaukee, WI	350	$1,423,000	($889,000)	$10,750,000	$30,714	7.55 (1.34 on a stabi-lized basis)		1/26/1996

2. Target Name: *Golden Park*

Description: Golden Park is a 72-unit senior housing community. Historically operated as a congregate care facility, ESC (the buyer) plans to refurbish it for use as an assisted living facility.

Comparison with ORP: Poor location comparison. Per bed purchase price may be considered relevant, as ORP facilities may need modification to accommodate bathrooms.

Location	Beds	Revenue	Net Income	Acquisition Price	Price Per Bed	Price/ Revenue	Cap	Transaction Date
San Bernardino, CA	72	$558,290	N/A	N/A	$29,167	3.76		N/A

3. Target Name: *Buena Vista Nursing Center*

Terms: $2.675 million in cash; $200,000 in a deferred note, payment of which depends on meeting certain financial targets.

Description: Buena Vista has 64 skilled nursing beds and 22 assisted living beds.

Comparison with ORP: Mix of assisted living and skilled nursing makes this a poor to average comparable. Smaller number of units compares favorably.

Location	Beds	Revenue	Net Income	Acquisition Price	Price Per Bed	Price/ Revenue	Cap	Transaction Date
Lexington, NC	86	N/A	N/A	$2.875 million	$33,430	N/A		1/26/1996

4. Target Name: *Northgate Park*

Terms: Cash

Description: A 126-unit independent living facility with 96% occupancy. Northgate earned $524,000 on revenue of $1,792,199.

Comparison with ORP: Single large facility with strong earnings. Upper end of price range.

Location	Beds	Revenue	Net Income	Acquisition Price	Price Per Bed	Price/ Revenue	Cap	Transaction Date
Cincinnati, OH	126	$1,792,199	$524,000	$7,500,000	$59,524	4.18	14.31	9/11/1996

Location	Beds	Revenue	Net Income	Acquisition Price	Price Per Bed	Price/ Revenue	Cap	Transaction Date

5. Target Name: *Four assisted living facilities*

Terms: Cash

Description: Four assisted living facilities with a total of 120 units.

Comparison with ORP: Smaller unit size compares favorably to ORP. However, lack of financial information diminishes comparable value.

Location	Beds	Revenue	Net Income	Acquisition Price	Price Per Bed	Price/ Revenue	Cap	Transaction Date
WI	120	N/A	N/A	$5,500,000	$45,833	N/A		12/26/1996

6. Target Name: *Matloon Health Care Center*

Terms: $5 million cash and $1.66 million note.

Description: Owned and operated by an individual since opening in 1978. Owner was retiring. There were 293 square feet per bed.

Comparison with ORP: Large number of units per facility. Square feet per bed was superior to ORP. Only 34% private pay census, comparing unfavorably to ORP.

Location	Beds	Revenue	Net Income	Acquisition Price	Price Per Bed	Price/ Revenue	Cap	Transaction Date
Matloon, IL	148	N/A	N/A	$6,660,000	$45,000	N/A	13.2	3/1996

7. Target Name: *Governors Park*

Description: State-of-the-art facility built in 1986. Located in an affluent area. At time of sale: 85% census; 75 skilled and 75 intermediate beds.

Comparison with ORP: Skilled and intermediate beds make it an average to poor comparable.

Location	Beds	Revenue	Net Income	Acquisition Price	Price Per Bed	Price/ Revenue	Cap	Transaction Date
Barrington, IL	150	N/A	N/A	$9,500,000	$66,500		12.1	11/1995

Source: ASLC appraisal dated 9/19/1997

Opinion of Value. The Opinion of Value of the properties of ASLC ranged from $8,200,000 to $8,900,000 on a fully stabilized basis. The properties' value ranged from $7,000,000 to $7,600,000 on an "as is" basis. This Opinion of Value was conducted by an outside appraisal company on September 19, 1997, and was used as a benchmark to help assess the final sales price of the company.

Actual Sale Information. After an analysis of the Opinion of Value was completed and other pricing considerations were taken into account, ASLC was listed for sale in October 1997 for $9,700,000. ASLC received 10 inquiries and 3 offers over the next five months. An offer was accepted from two groups, which split the operations of ASLC into "the CBRF package" and "Wilkinson Woods." The Kingswood Place program was shut down, and a "liquidated damages" clause was exercised, costing ASLC $330,000 over a two-year period. The CBRF package, consisting of the seven CBRF programs, was sold for $4,100,000 in cash, with the sale closing on June 30, 1998. Wilkinson Woods closed shortly thereafter at a sale price of $1,900,000 in cash for a total sales price of $6,000,000, less sales commissions.

Analysis By Chapter

Chapter 1 – The History of Disability. With the occurrence of the industrial revolution in the early 1900s, for the first time in human existence, the family unit was going to change forever. In agrarian societies, the elderly were cared for by family or passed away before needing assisted living services. As the 20th century drew to a close, the family unit had become fragmented, with people living in all parts of the country. This occurred at the same time that life spans of the elderly were increasing dramatically, mainly due to technological and medical advancements. These changes in the way we live provided the opening for the elderly services industry to flourish. Society evolved from families caring for their frail elderly to nursing home care to care in retirement communities and other community-based settings. The days of the nursing home being the only care alternative were over by the early 1990s, and the assisted living industry seized the moment. An industry was born, and they thought they were specially equipped as a company to succeed in it.

Discussion question: Given this history, what type of organization or industry do you believe is best equipped to operate in the assisted living market space?

Chapter 2 – Important Cases, Laws, and Watershed Events. The elderly services industry benefited from the hard-fought gains of the civil rights movement, the disabilities movement, and the laws that paved the way as explained in Chapter 2 of the text. Licensing, Medicaid Waivers, block grant money, and legal rights for the elderly paved the way for a more consumer-friendly, community-based system of care. The elderly became a protected class with rights protecting their fundamental needs. As a company that specialized in programming and meeting the needs of society's most vulnerable population, they believed they fit in this market space due to their unique competencies and familiarity with this market terrain.

Discussion question: Name two specific disability laws, cases, or events that you think had the strongest positive effect on the elderly services arena.

Chapter 4 – Agency Mission. They were a human services company whose mission was directed squarely towards providing services for individuals with disabilities. Is being elderly or aged a disability? That is open for debate. To be sure, there are similarities. At that time, they took the view that the elderly services arena was an adjacent business space. It required many of the services they were expert at providing, it involved caring for some of society's most vulnerable individuals, and it had the usual daily rate and occupancy battles that they were used to launching every day in the disabilities arena. Over time, it became apparent that they had engaged in "mission creep." It was not going to work over the long haul for them to be operating in the elderly services market space.

Discussion question: In what ways was the voyage into ASLC an example of mission creep?

_____

_____

_____

_____

_____

Discussion question: In what two ways was it a smart strategy for ORP?

_____

_____

_____

_____

_____

Discussion question: In what two ways could it be perceived as an unwise move?

_____

_____

_____

_____

_____

Chapter 6 – Organizational Structure. They set up the ASLC organization structure in a similar fashion to the human services companies they were running, using program managers and professionals at each site who had experience working with people with disabilities. They believed the program composition and quality would be more important than the glitz of real estate brick and mortar or the empty promises of real estate developers. They staffed the programs with human services professionals, each of whom had experience working with people with disabilities, and adopted many of the policies and procedures for coverage, medications, and meals. Their sales and marketing groups were also comprised of human services professionals.

Discussion question: In what three ways do the core competencies of quality programming in the disabilities services area match well with the assisted living industry?

_____

_____

_____

_____

_____

_____

Discussion question: In what three ways is it a mismatch?

_____

_____

_____

_____

_____

_____

Chapter 7 – Corporate Culture and Exceptional Leadership. The corporate culture was healthy. Human service professionals "pulled the rope in the same direction," operated with integrity, and acted responsibly, just as one would expect from a human services company operating a program. Individuals that resided in the assisted living facilities were generally very satisfied and considered the services a great value—but only if they truly needed the care and other services that were being provided (sometimes mandated by licensing).

Discussion question: In what ways does the senior market need quality human service programming?

_____

_____

_____

_____

_____

_____

_____

Chapter 8 – Licensing and Rule-Making Authorities. Assisted living operations ran the gamut from totally unlicensed operations to highly regulated CBRFs. Unlicensed operations lacked the "DNA" that revolved around licensing responsibilities, treatment and care, resident rights, the physical environment, and safety. These unlicensed operations had the lowest cost. Licensing requirements were often onerous. The licensed operations tended to require services that the elderly market often needed but did not want (a difference in perception). Sometimes the reluctance was financial, such as for transportation services (perhaps they could still drive) or meal programs required by the CBRF code (perhaps they only wanted to purchase breakfast not three meals a day).

Discussion question: When should a human services company operate unlicensed programs that do not contain the "DNA" of its mission?

_____

_____

_____

_____

Discussion question: When should a human services company operate a program in a licensed setting that contains a mismatch between market wants and licensing requirements?

_____

_____

_____

_____

Chapter 9 – Opening a New Program. Identifying the right value proposition in the elderly services arena is difficult for a human services company because the perception of the need by the agency is different from the perception of the need by the prospective resident. Residents have many choices, and pricing decisions are very elastic. Future clients wait too long to consider placement and reach the point that their health has deteriorated, placing stress on staffing. The location is very important, as transportation routes, shopping, a safe environment, and aesthetics rule the day. Cumulative start-up losses were significant for some programs, with breakeven (about 15 beds) taking a few years to occur in some cases. Placements generally happened at a slower pace than the typical human services program for people with disabilities, perhaps due to the different nature of the marketing and sales skills needed for the elderly market versus the disability market. Compared to a typical disabilities program, the assisted living program featured a slower start-up revenue ramp, a longer payback, a lower return on investment, and higher client turnover as the health of many residents deteriorated.

Discussion question: Assume your company operated in the disabilities arena; make an argument FOR expanding into the assisted living market space.

_____

_____

_____

_____

_____

_____

Discussion question: Make an argument AGAINST expanding into the assisted living market space.

_____

_____

_____

_____

_____

Chapter 10 – Normalized Operations. One of the significant differences between serving individuals with disabilities and non-disabled elderly adults was resident turnover. The turnover at ASLC always kept them scrambling for census and made it harder to achieve their contribution margin goals. While the intake process was similar for the two populations, the elderly tended to come in too late and left too early. The length of stay was similar to children in a residential school setting, in the 1- to 2-year range, with the intensity of service rising rapidly towards the end of placement. Adults with disabilities often were in the system for a lifetime, sometimes spanning 30 years or more, requiring stable care needs over that duration. The "lifetime revenue" that could be expected from an individual in the elderly market was significantly less than one would think. In addition, they found that they were "over serving" the elderly market. Although the market liked and grew to expect the services of the brand promise, which placed an emphasis on quality programming and care, it did not want to pay for those extra services. The elderly market was generally more interested in perception than in the substance of the service offering.

Discussion question: How does the "lifetime revenue" of a client affect a program's contribution margin?

_____

_____

_____

_____

_____

Discussion question: If you were in charge of ORP revenue growth strategies and were determined to open programs in the senior market, how would you justify this to management?

_____

_____

_____

_____

_____

Chapter 16 – Sales, Marketing, and Generating Revenue. Marketing is the science of driving sales by matching the needs of a customer with the skills of the organization. Given the number of elderly people, one might think that referrals and sales would be plentiful. That turned out not to be the case. Only a small sliver of the market potential became "eligible" for ASLC programs—needed the personal care and hands-on services that they offered—and an even smaller number were willing to pay for these services. By far the largest portion of the elderly market did not want to move out of their homes at all and preferred that services be provided in the confines of their current residence. Generally, a triangle of dysfunction was present and its players were: (1) the prospective resident (who needed placement), (2) a significant other (child, spouse, or friend who wanted the placement), and (3) the provider (ASLC). Services were 50% private pay and 50% came from the community options program (COP). There tended to be less drama involving COP and more when the payer was a private pay. COP referrals were more targeted, resulting in a higher likelihood that a referral would turn into a placement. Private pay closings were generally driven by need, but those residents were extremely cost-conscious, many times unrealistically so. This private pay dynamic was new for human services professionals, and they struggled with it each day from opening to sale.

Discussion question: Provide three examples of how marketing, sales, and generating revenue are different between the private pay market and the government market.

Discussion question: Provide two examples of how the marketing and sales functions differ when operating in the seniors market versus the disabilities marketplace.

Chapter 17 – Pricing. ASLC offered a distinctive service in a commodity market. That is, they offered services driven by needs when prices were driven by the glut of suppliers. The elderly services industry attracted every Tom, Dick, and Harry who thought they were going to make vast fortunes from the aging of America. Real estate developers, nursing home chains, hospitals, moms and pops, religious orders, municipalities, health care providers, and human services companies—all thought their future fortunes were going to come from serving seniors. In a way, this made sense because seniors represented 20% of the population and controlled 80% of the wealth in this country. As a human services company, however, when it came to marketing and pricing, ASLC was out of its league. ASLC did not price below contribution margin, but they had difficulty fine-tuning rates for maximum profits. They could not determine price elasticity because there was a dizzying array of alternatives in the marketplace. Deception about the scope of service delivery (personal care, meals, medication) was rampant. It is fair to say that ASLC was never able to understand fully the essence of the price effect versus unit of service effect. Consequently, in a typical month, ASLC may have left significant amounts of money on the table.

Discussion question: What would you have done to minimize the effect of "leaving money on the table?"

Chapter 18 – Profit from the Core. It is essential to the success of any human services company to identify and introduce new programs that will generate profits and enhance other service offerings. ASLC was an "adjacent business opportunity" for the parent company that specialized in providing human service programming for individuals with disabilities in various settings. By applying its core competencies (providing personal care, housing, and behavior management for individuals with disabilities) to the new emerging elderly services market, they thought they would find utopia! The human services business is always precarious and depends on political winds, legislation, economy, government funding, and public policy for its very existence. What if the parent company could take its skills into the world of private pay—into a world of demographics that almost defied comprehension and away from the idiosyncrasies of government funding? Who wouldn't want to do that? The assisted living industry was a first circle adjacency. It required a common skill set to the human services delivery necessary for people with disabilities. ORP thought they had a winner. But, the first rule of profit from the core is "focus on your core business, and seek to build it to its full potential." ORP did not do that, and they may have made a fundamental mistake that violated its mission of serving people with disabilities. Aging is not a disability; it is just a result of the calendar moving through months and years.

Discussion question: Can you think of any instance where ORP could have expanded successfully into some segment of the elderly services arena?

Chapter 23 – Real Estate. ASLC had three property options: renting, purchasing an existing building, or building new. Location was the most important factor in determining where to open programs. Building was out of the question because lead times were long, and they wanted to be located in certain established urban areas. Pricing became secondary (within reason) because they thought location was correlated to a high census and high daily rates that could overcome higher occupancy costs.

The big problem for cash flow was that every program location required a significant influx of cash at the start. In the early 1990s, the cost of the average apartment building (their equipment) was $300,000. That could be financed at 80% loan-to-fair-market value, generating $240,000. Net cash required at closing was about 22% (which included $6,000 closing costs) or $66,000. Then came the building renovations to get the building fit for purpose. These costs were generally in the 50–60% range, or about $165,000. In addition, the apartment buildings needed to be off line before renovation could start. This period included a phase-down of rental income and time during construction where no revenue could be generated. These operating losses could approach another $100,000 (before tax effects). So the cash investment required to get the property fit for occupancy was $300,000 for the building, $6,000 for closing costs, $165,000 for renovations, and $100,000 for the rent phase-down, for a total of $571,000. Factoring in the $240,000 mortgage financing resulted in a $331,000 net cash outlay per building. This was only for the property. There were also costs for furnishings and equipment, plus start-up losses to get to breakeven once operations commenced. One last thing: the renovations added no FMV to the building. It was arguably worth LESS than the $300,000 paid because it was not rentable in its post-construction condition as apartments.

Discussion question: Can you think of two ways ASLC could have reduced the cash required for start-up?

Chapter 25 – Business Valuation. Businesses in different industries can be valued differently even though they have the same EBITDA. Businesses are generally valued using a blend of three approaches: (1) the income, (2) the market, and (3) the asset approach. While the income and the asset approaches are basically math problems, the market approach can vary from industry to industry. All else being equal, the market multiples that investors were paying for human services companies were lower than the multiples investors were paying for assisted living companies and other related business in the "senior" industry. This price differential was largely driven by the fact that banks were lending more money with better terms to borrowers in the senior housing industry in the 1990s, and more investors were interested in this sector, which helped mitigate the entry costs ASLC incurred.

Discussion question: Do you think the difference in market multiples between the human services industry and the seniors assisted living industry was justified? Please explain your answer.

Chapter 28 – The Future. Although ASLC was, at best, a breakeven proposition when it was sold in 1998, the industry is very different today. What would have happened to ASLC if they had continued operations? Would the balance between the political parties, which is essential to the health of a delivery system, have affected the environment of ASLC? Would longer life spans, economic conditions on the ground, a shortage of qualified employees, and limited financing alternatives strangle the industry? All of this is open to debate. Was the sale a good decision or a bad decision for the overall company?

Discussion question: Given what you have learned here, do you think it was a wise decision for ASLC human services company to exit the senior assisted living industry?

Discussion question: If not, what are three things that management might have missed in its analysis?

ASLC EXHIBIT #1

Marjorie Home
Adjusted Historical Financials

	1994	Adjustmts	Adjusted 1994	% Rev	1995	Adjustments	Adjusted 1995	% Rev	1996	Adjustments	Adjusted 1996	% Rev	Six months ended 6/97	Adjustments	Adj 6/97	% Rev	Nrml Avg(1)	Base Year (2)	% Rev
# of Units	20				20				20				20					20	
Revenue/Unit/Year	$19,464				$21,143				$23,464				$23,675				$14.3k-23.2k (2)	$24,924	
Occupancy %	100%				100%				100%				95%					90%	
GROSS POT. INCOME																		$498,480	
VACANCY RESERVE																		(49,848)	
EFFECTIVE GROSS INCOME	$389,872		$389,872		$422,851		$422,851		$475,204		$475,204		$226,754		$226,754			$448,632	
EXPENSES (4)																			
G&A (5)	$62,929	($23,392)	$39,537	10%	$81,956	($27,403)	$54,553	13%	$131,167	($39,824)	$91,343	19%	$51,374	($23,486)	$27,888	12%	10%	$56,891	13%
Dietary	39,282		39,282	10%	35,749		35,749	8%	40,665		40,665	9%	21,663		21,663	10%	11%	44,193	10%
Housekeeping & Laundry	12,479		12,479	3%	13,831		13,831	3%	9,317		9,317	2%	6,599		6,599	3%	3%	13,461	3%
Personal Care	139,856		139,856	36%	163,619		163,619	39%	143,235		143,235	30%	73,983		73,983	33%	20%	150,924	34%
Ancillary	8,688		8,688	2%	13,510		13,510	3%	3,329		3,329	1%	2,156		2,156	1%	3%	4,398	1%
Depreciation	3,339	(3,339)	0	0%	3,692	(3,692)	0	0%	3,906	(3,906)	0	0%	2,121	(2,121)	0	0%	NA	0	0%
Property (6)	88,536	754	89,290	23%	96,180	204	96,384	23%	102,208	(10,896)	91,312	19%	52,694	(6,108)	46,586	21%	10%	95,035	21%
Management Fee (5)	0	23,392	23,392	6%	0	25,371	25,371	6%	0	28,512	28,512	6%	0	13,605	13,605	6%	6%	26,918	6%
Total Expenses	$355,108		$352,523		$408,538		$403,018		$433,828		$407,715		$210,590		$192,479			$391,821	
Expense per Unit			$17,626				$20,151				$20,386				$19,248			$19,591	
EBITDA	$34,764		$37,349	10%	$14,313		$19,833	5%	$41,476		$67,489	14%	$16,164		$34,274	15%	19%-35%(2)	$56,811	13%

Method	Rate	Value-Business	Value-Real Estate(7)	Total Value	Value/Unit
Capitalization Rate	12.0%	$473,000	$459,000	$932,000	$46,600
Capitalization Rate	13.0%	$437,000	$424,000	$861,000	$43,050
Effective Gross Income Multipliers	1.35			$606,000	$30,300

Notes
(1) Average based on "Assisted Living Development Cost Survey", 1997, Capital Research Group.
(2) Information based on "The State of Seniors Housing 1995, Americans Senior Housing Assoc. and Coopers & Lybrand LLP." Range represents Lower Quartile to Upper Quartile.
(3) Base year revenue/unit/year is based on actual December 1996 average revenue per resident.
(4) Employees benefits were allocated to various expense categories based on averages from "Assisted Living Development Cost Survey", 1997.
(5) ORP allocates properties 6% of EGI for corporate overhead, including accounting and legal fees. These charges have been recast from G&A to management fees. Salaries and benefits relating to the marketing department have been eliminated.
(6) The property is owned and leased to ORP in a non arm's length transaction. Property expense has been recast to provide for a 12% return on fair market value of real estate. Fair market value of the real estate improvements was based on information from the tax assessors office. The annual lease rate for this property was estimated at $55,104.
(7) Real estate value was derived from capitalizing the property's estimated annual lease rate of $55,104 at the cap rate shown.

Exhibit 1, Page 1

Wabash Home
Adjusted Historical Financials

	1994	Adjustments	Adjusted 1994	% Rev	1995	Adjustments	Adjusted 1995	% Rev	1996	Adjustments	Adjusted 1996	% Rev	Six months ended 6/97	Adjustments	Adj 6/97	% Rev	Ntnl Avg(1)	Base Year (3)	% Rev
# of Units	20				20				20				20					20	
Revenue/Unit/Year	$16,641				$18,657				$21,335				$20,249		$20,697		$14,3k,23,24 (2)	$22,824	
Occupancy %	85%				90%				95%				90%				94%	90%	
GROSS POT. INCOME:																			
VACANCY RESERVE																		$456,480	15%
																		(45,648)	
EFFECTIVE GROSS INCOME	$332,818		$332,818		$373,141		$373,141		$426,703		$426,703		$202,493		$202,493			$410,832	
EXPENSES (4)																			
G&A (5)	$54,085	($19,969)	$34,116	10%	$78,013	($24,421)	$53,593	14%	$141,280	($36,914)	$94,366	22%	$51,883	($22,031)	$29,852	15%	10%	$60,899	15%
Dietary	38,932		38,932	12%	40,861		40,861	11%	39,718		39,718	9%	19,616		19,616	10%	11%	40,017	10%
Housekeeping & Laundry	15,829		15,829	5%	21,372		21,372	6%	9,234		9,234	2%	7,279		7,279	4%	3%	14,849	4%
Personal Care	147,607		147,607	44%	161,721		161,721	43%	150,228		150,228	35%	77,502		77,502	38%	20%	158,105	38%
Ancillary	16,887		16,887	5%	10,674		10,674	3%	4,889		4,889	1%	2,880		2,880	1%	3%	5,875	1%
Depreciation	233	(233)	0	0%	2,290	(2,290)	0	0%	3,462	(3,462)	0	0%	1,897	(1,897)	0	0%	NA	0	0%
Property (6)	72,614	(11,300)	61,314	18%	75,157	(11,769)	63,388	17%	68,506	(12,248)	56,258	13%	39,541	(6,339)	33,202	16%	10%	67,732	16%
Management Fee (5)	0	19,969	19,969	6%	0	22,388	22,388	6%	0	25,602	25,602	6%	0	12,150	12,150	6%	6%	24,650	6%
Total Expenses	$346,187		$334,654		$390,088		$373,997		$407,317		$380,296		$200,599		$182,481			$372,262	
Expense per Unit			$16,733				$18,700				$19,015				$18,248			$18,613	
EBITDA	($13,369)		($1,836)	-1%	($16,947)		($856)	-0%	$19,386		$46,407	11%	$1,895		$20,012	10%	19%-35%(2)	$38,570	9%

VALUATION

Method	Rate		Value-Business(7)	Value-Real Estate	Total Value	Value/Unit
Capitalization Rate	12.0%		$321,000	$275,000	$596,000	$29,800
Capitalization Rate	13.0%		$297,000	$253,000	$550,000	$27,500
Effective Gross Income Multipliers	1.35				$555,000	$27,750

Notes

(1) Average based on "Assisted Living Development Cost Survey", 1997, Capital Research Group.

(2) Information based on "The State of Seniors Housing 1995, Americans Senior Housing Assoc. and Coopers & Lybrand LLP."
Range represents Lower Quartile to Upper Quartile

(3) Base year revenue/unit/year is based on actual December 1996 average revenue per resident.

(4) Employees benefits were allocated to various expense categories based on averages from "Assisted Living Development Cost Survey", 1997.

(5) ORP allocates properties 6% of EGI for corporate overhead, including accounting and legal fees. These charges have been recast from G&A to management fees.
Salaries and benefits relating to the marketing department have been eliminated

(6) The property is owned and leased to ORP in a non arm's-length transaction. Property expense has been recast to provide for a 12% return on fair market value of real estate.
Fair market value of the real estate improvements was based on information from the tax assessors office. The annual lease rate for this property was estimated at $32,940.

Fardale
Adjusted Historical Financials

	1994	Adjustments	Adjusted 1994	% Rev	1995	Adjustments	Adjusted 1995	% Rev	1996	Adjustments	Adjusted 1996	% Rev	6/97	Adjustments	Adj 6/97	% Rev	Unit Avg.(1)	Base Year(3)	% Rev
# of Units	20				20				20				20					20	
Revenue/Unit/Year	$18,709				$19,899				$22,599				$23,719				$14,1k-24,2k (2)	$22,724	
Occupancy %	85%				95%				100%				100%				94%	90%	
GROSS POT. INCOME			$374,171				$397,989				$451,978				$247,192			$474,480	
VACANCY RESERVE																		(47,448)	
EFFECTIVE GROSS INCOME	$374,171				$397,989				$451,978				$247,192		$237,192			$427,032	
EXPENSES (4)																			
G&A (5)	$60,887	($22,450)	$38,436	10%	$80,416	($25,911)	$54,504	14%	$131,092	($38,430)	$92,662	21%	$52,046	($24,113)	$27,938	12%	10%	$56,988	13%
Dietary	39,228		39,228	10%	38,989		38,989	10%	39,804		39,804	9%	39,804		22,718	10%	11%	46,344	11%
Housekeeping & Laundry	10,945		10,945	3%	14,496		14,496	4%	7,707		7,707	2%	6,391		6,391	3%	3%	13,037	3%
Personal Care	126,144		126,144	34%	139,516		139,516	35%	140,183		140,183	31%	72,274		72,274	30%	20%	147,438	35%
Ancillary	13,176		13,176	4%	10,451		10,451	3%	4,635		4,635	1%	2,634		2,634	1%	3%	5,374	1%
Depreciation	1,507	(1,507)	0	0%	2,418	(2,418)	0	0%	2,674	(2,674)	0	0%	1,422	(1,422)	0	0%	NA	0	0%
Property (6)	74,258	(4,134)	70,134	19%	81,524	(4,509)	77,015	19%	73,521	(4,974)	68,547	15%	37,464	(2,712)	34,752	15%	10%	70,895	17%
Management Fee (5)	0	22,450	22,450	6%	0	23,879	23,879	6%	0	27,119	27,119	6%	0	14,232	14,232	6%	6%	25,622	6%
Total Expenses	$326,344		$320,503		$367,809		$358,850		$399,616		$380,657		$194,951		$180,935			$365,698	
Expense per Unit			$16,025				$17,943				$19,033				$18,094			$18,285	
EBITDA	$48,027		$53,668	14%	$30,179		$39,139	10%	$52,362		$71,322	16%	$42,241		$56,257	24%	19%-35% (2)	$61,334	14%

VALUATION

Method	Rate		Value	Value-Real Estate (7)	Total Value	Value/Unit
Capitalization Rate	12.0%		$511,000	$325,000	$836,000	$41,800
Capitalization Rate	13.0%		$472,000	$300,000	$772,000	$38,600
Effective Gross Income Multipliers	1.35				$576,000	$28,800

Notes
(1) Average based on "Assisted Living Development Cost Survey", 1997, Capital Research Group.
(2) Information based on "The State of Seniors Housing 1995, Americans Senior Housing Assoc. and Coopers & Lybrand LLP."
   Range represents Lower Quartile to Upper Quartile
(3) Base Year revenue/unit/year is based on actual December 1996 average revenue per resident. With the exception of management fees and property, Base Year expenses are based on annualized adjusted 6/97 expenses and adjusted 2% for inflation
(4) Employees benefits were allocated to various expense categories based on averages from "Assisted Living Development Cost Survey", 1997
(5) ORP allocates properties 6% of EGI for corporate overhead, including accounting and legal fees. These charges have been recast from G&A to management fees.
   Salaries and benefits relating to the marketing department have been eliminated.
(6) The property is owned and leased to ORP in a non arm's-length transaction. Property expense has been recast to provide for a 12% return on fair market value of real estate.
   Fair market value of the real estate improvements was based on information from the tax assessor's office. The annual lease rate for this property was estimated at $39,036.
(7) Real estate value was derived from capitalizing the property's estimated annual lease rate of $39,036 at the cap rate shown.

Exhibit 1, Page 3

Michele Home
Adjusted Historical Financials

	1994	Adjustments	Adjusted 1994	% Rev	1995	Adjustment	Adjusted 1995	% Rev	1996	Adjustments	Adjusted 1996	% Rev	Six months ended 6/97	Adjustments	Adj 6/97	% Rev	Natl Avg(1)	Base Year	% Rev
# of Units	20				20				20				20				20	20	
Revenue/Unit/Year	$19,559				$20,504				$17,342				$26,529				$14,3k-24,2k(2)	$28,980 (3)	
Occupancy %	100%				80%				95%				75%					90%	
GROSS POT. INCOME																		$579,600	
VACANCY RESERVE																		(57,960)	
EFFECTIVE GROSS INCOME	$391,177				$410,088				$346,833				$265,290		$265,290			$521,640	
EXPENSES (4)																			
G&A (5)	$61,391	($23,471)	$37,920	10%	$85,771	($26,637)	$59,133	14%	$138,556	($32,122)	$106,434	31%	$56,699	($25,799)	$30,900	12%	10%	$63,036	12%
Dietary	34,747		34,747	9%	37,506		37,506	9%	31,828		31,828	9%	19,945		19,945	8%	11%	40,687	8%
Housekeeping & Laundry	12,648		12,648	3%	11,891		11,891	3%	12,612		12,612	4%	6,869		6,869	3%	3%	14,012	3%
Personal Care	138,823		138,823	35%	159,247		159,247	39%	173,170		173,170	50%	97,468		97,468	37%	20%	198,835	38%
Ancillary	14,884		14,884	4%	15,722		15,722	4%	10,270		10,270	3%	5,907		5,907	2%	3%	12,051	2%
Depreciation	916	(916)	0	0%	1,419	(1,419)	0	0%	8,530	(8,530)	0	0%	5,893	(5,893)	0	0%	NA	0	0%
Property (6)	71,335	(6,986)	64,349	16%	72,518	(7,538)	64,980	16%	81,517	(19,620)	61,897	18%	40,310	(10,356)	29,954	11%	10%	61,105	12%
Management Fee (5)	0	23,471	23,471	6%	0	24,605	24,605	6%	0	20,810	20,810	6%	0	15,917	15,917	6%	6%	31,298	6%
Total Expenses	$334,744		$326,842		$384,074		$373,085		$456,483		$417,021		$233,090		$206,960			$422,198	
Expense per Unit			$16,342				$18,654				$20,851				$20,696			$21,110	
EBITDA	$56,433		$64,335	16%	$26,014		$37,003	9%	($109,650)		($70,189)	20%	$32,200		$58,330	22%		$99,442	19%

VALUATION

Method	Rate	Value–Business(7)	Value–Real Estate	Value/Unit	Total Value
Capitalization Rate	12.0%	$829,000	$291,000	$56,000	$1,120,000
Capitalization Rate	13.0%	$765,000	$269,000	$51,700	$1,034,000
Effective Gross Income Multipliers	1.35			$35,200	$704,000

Notes

(1) Average based on "Assisted Living Development Cost Survey", 1997, Capital Research Group.
(2) Information based on "The State of Seniors Housing 1995, Americans Senior Housing Assoc. and Coopers & Lybrand LLP"
   Range represents Lower Quartile to Upper Quartile.
(3) Base year revenue/unit/year is based on actual December 1996 average revenue per resident.
(4) Employees benefits were allocated to various expense categories based on averages from "Assisted Living Development Cost Survey", 1997.
(5) ORP allocates properties 6% of EGI for corporate overhead, including accounting and legal fees. These charges have been recast from G&A to management fees.
   Salaries and benefits relating to the marketing department have been eliminated.
(6) The property is owned and leased to ORP in a non arm's-length transaction. Property expense has been recast to provide for a 12% return on fair market value of real estate. Fair market value of
   fair market value of the real estate improvements was based on information from the tax assessor's office. The annual lease rate for this property was estimated at $34,920.
(7) Real estate value was derived from capitalizing the property's estimated annual lease rate of $34,920 at the cap rate shown.

Exhibit 1, Page 4

Sunnyridge Home
Adjusted Historical Financials

	1994	Adjustments	Adjusted 1994	% Rev	1995	Adjustments	Adjusted 1995	% Rev	1996	Adjustments	Adjusted 1996	% Rev	Six months ended 6/97	Adjustments	Adj 6/92	% Rev	Ntnl Avg(1)	Base Year (4)	% Rev	Stabilized Base Year (2)	% Rev
# of Units (2)	16		16		16		16		16		16		16		16			16		20	
Revenue/Unit/Year	$21,147				$27,646				$25,807				$24,092				$14,4-21,2(4)	$24,612		$24,612	
Occupancy %	100%				95%				80%				75%					90%		90%	
GROSS POT. INCOME																					
VACANCY RESERVE																		$393,792		$492,240	
																		(39,379)		(49,224)	
EFFECTIVE GROSS INCOME	$338,664		$338,664		$442,337		$442,337		$412,915		$412,915		$192,732		$192,732			$354,413		$443,016	
EXPENSES (5)																					
G&A (6)	$58,018	($20,320)	$37,698	11%	$82,219	($28,072)	$54,147	12%	$138,564	($36,087)	$102,477	25%	$49,695	($21,445)	$28,250	15%	10%	$57,629	16%	$57,629	13%
Dietary	35,781		35,781	11%	36,349		36,349	8%	39,202		39,202	9%	18,931		18,931	10%	11%	38,620	11%	38,620	9%
Housekeeping & Laundry	13,993		13,993	4%	12,216		12,216	3%	6,679		6,679	2%	6,324		6,324	3%	3%	12,902	4%	12,902	3%
Personal Care	132,855		132,855	39%	152,034		152,034	34%	145,817		145,817	35%	64,301		64,301	34%	20%	131,174	37%	131,174	30%
Ancillary	15,340		15,340	5%	16,327		16,327	4%	12,468		12,468	3%	5,198		5,198	3%	3%	10,604	3%	10,604	2%
Depreciation	3,766	(3,766)	0	0%	4,066	(4,066)	0	0%	4,337	(4,337)	0	0%	2,245	(2,245)	0	NA		0	0%	0	0%
Property (7)	83,430	(16,876)	66,554	20%	86,931	(17,426)	69,505	16%	78,968	(18,026)	60,942	15%	41,207	(9,288)	31,919	17%	10%	65,116	18%	65,116	15%
Management Fee (5)	0	20,320	20,320	6%	0	26,540	26,540	6%	0	24,775	24,775	6%	0	11,564	11,564	6%	6%	21,265	6%	26,581	6%
Total Expenses	$343,172		$322,530		$390,642		$367,118		$426,035		$392,360		$187,902		$166,488			$337,310		$342,626	
Expense per Unit			$20,158				$22,945				$24,523				$20,811			$21,082		$17,131	
EBITDA	($4,508)		$16,134	5%	$51,695		$75,219	17%	($13,120)		$20,555	5%	$4,830		$26,244	14%	19%-35%(3)	$17,103	5%	$100,390	23%

VALUATION-Base Year

Method	Rate	Value-Business(8)	Value-Real Estate	Total Value	Value/Unit
Capitalization Rate	12.0%	$143,000	$294,000	$437,000	$27,313
Capitalization Rate	13.0%	$132,000	$272,000	$404,000	$25,250
Effective Gross Income Multipliers	1.35			$478,000	$29,875

VALUATION-Stabilized Year

Method	Rate	Value-Business(8)	Value-Real Estate	Total Value	Value/Unit
Capitalization Rate	12.0%	$837,000	$294,000	$1,131,000	$56,550
Capitalization Rate	13.0%	$772,000	$272,000	$1,044,000	$52,200
Effective Gross Income Multipliers	1.35			$598,000	$29,900

Notes
(1) Average based on "Assisted Living Development Cost Survey", 1997, Capital Research Group.
(2) Four offices are currently occupying four units; for this valuation it is anticipated these will be converted back to rentable units.
(3) Information based on "The State of Seniors Housing 1995, Americans Senior Housing Assoc. and Coopers & Lybrand LLP."
Range represents Lower Quartile to Upper Quartile
(4) Base year revenue/unit/year is based on actual December 1996 average revenue per resident.
(5) Employees' benefits were allocated to various expense categories based on averages from "Assisted Living Development Cost Survey", 1997.
(6) ORP allocates properties 6% of EGI for corporate overhead, including accounting and legal fees. These charges have been recast from G&A to management fees. Salaries and benefits relating to the marketing department have been eliminated.
(7) The property is owned and leased to ORP in a non arms-length transaction. Property expense has been recast to provide for a 12% return on fair market value of real estate. Fair market value of the real estate improvements was based on information from the tax assessors office. The annual lease rate for this property was estimated at $35,304.
(8) Real estate value was derived from capitalizing the property's estimated annual lease rate of $35,104 at the cap rate shown.

Grantosa
Adjusted Historical Financials

	1994	Adjustments	Adjusted 1994	% Rev	1995	Adjustments	Adjusted 1995	% Rev	1996	Adjustments	Adjusted 1996	% Rev	Six months ended 6/97	Adjustments	Adj 6/97	% Rev	Ntnl Avg[1]	Base Year	% Rev
# of Units	20		20		20		20		20		20		20		20			20	
Revenue/Unit/Year	$20,400				$21,290				$23,832				$23,698				$14.3k-23.2k (2)	$24,720 (3)	
Occupancy %	95%				95%				100%				100%					90%	
GROSS POT. INCOME																		$494,400	
VACANCY RESERVE																		(49,440)	
EFFECTIVE GROSS INCOME			$408,900				$425,800		$476,637		$476,637		$246,979		$246,979			$444,960	
EXPENSES (4)																			
G&A (5)	$56,911	($24,534)	$32,377	8%	$80,992	($27,580)	$53,412	13%	$138,681	($39,910)	$98,771	21%	$55,980	($24,700)	$31,280	13%	10%	$63,811	14%
Dietary	42,600		42,600	10%	51,046		51,046	12%	58,484		58,484	12%	22,267		22,267	9%	11%	45,425	10%
Housekeeping & Laundry	14,041		14,041	3%	12,997		12,997	3%	9,036		9,036	2%	6,833		6,833	3%	3%	13,940	3%
Personal Care	138,418		138,418	34%	145,729		145,729	34%	151,004		151,004	32%	74,942		74,942	30%	20%	152,882	34%
Ancillary	10,292		10,292	3%	9,969		9,969	2%	6,322		6,322	1%	3,375		3,375	1%	3%	6,884	2%
Depreciation	8,222	(8,222)	0	0%	8,345	(8,345)	0	0%	8,695	(8,695)	0	0%	4,341	(4,341)	0	0%	NA	0	0%
Property (6)	76,875	(15,292)	61,583	15%	85,526	(15,452)	70,074	16%	74,719	(15,932)	58,787	12%	37,709	(8,126)	29,583	12%	10%	60,349	14%
Management Fee (5)	0	24,534	24,534	6%	0	25,548	25,548	6%	0	28,598	28,598	6%	0	14,819	14,819	6%	6%	26,698	6%
Total Expenses	$347,360		$323,846		$394,603		$368,773		$446,941		$411,002		$205,447		$183,099		19%-35%(2)	$373,521	
Expense per Unit			$16,192				$18,439				$20,550				$18,310			$18,676	
EBITDA	$61,540		$85,054	21%	$31,197		$57,027	13%	$29,696		$65,635	14%	$41,532		$63,880	26%		$71,439	16%

VALUATION

Method	Rate
Capitalization Rate	12.0%
Capitalization Rate	13.0%
Effective Gross Income Multipliers	1.35

Value-Business (7)	Value-Real Estate	Total Value	Value/Unit
$595,000	$294,000	$889,000	$44,450
$550,000	$272,000	$822,000	$41,100
		$601,000	$30,050

Notes
(1) Average based on "Assisted Living Development Cost Survey", 1997. Capital Research Group.
(2) Information based on "The State of Seniors Housing", 1995, Americans Senior Housing Assoc. and Coopers & Lybrand L.L.P."
  Range represents Lower Quartile to Upper Quartile.
(3) Base year revenue/unit/year is based on actual December 1996 average revenue per resident.
(4) Employees' benefits were allocated to various expense categories based on averages from "Assisted Living Development Cost Survey", 1997.
(5) ORP allocates properties 6% of EGI for corporate overhead, including accounting and legal fees. These charges have been recast from G&A to management fees.
  Salaries and benefits relating to the marketing department have been eliminated.
(6) The property is owned and leased to ORP in a non arm's-length transaction. Property expense has been recast to provide for a 12% return on fair market value of real estate.
  Fair market value of the real estate improvements was based on information from the tax assessors office. The annual lease rate for this property was estimated at $35,328.
(7) Real estate value was derived from capitalizing the property's estimated annual lease rate of $55,104 at the cap rate shown.

Marian Heights
Adjusted Historical Financials

	1994	Adjustments	Adjusted 1994	% Rev	1995	Adjustment	Adjusted 1995	% Rev	1996	Adjustments	Adjusted 1996	% Rev	Six months ended 6/97	Adjustments	Adj 6/97	% Rev	Nini Avg(1)	Base Year(3)	% Rev
# of Units	17				17				17				17					17	
Revenue/Unit/Year	$8,411				$20,257				$23,828				$24,149				$14.3K-21.2K(2)	$24,816	
Occupancy %	71%				82%				100%				94%					90%	
GROSS POT. INCOME																			
VACANCY RESERVE																			
EFFECTIVE GROSS INCOME	$142,981		$142,981		$344,370		$344,370		$405,074		$405,074		$205,266		$205,266			$379,085	
EXPENSES (4)																			
G&A (5)	$45,652	($8,579)	$37,073	26%	$76,173	($22,694)	$53,479	16%	$118,211	($35,616)	$82,595	20%	$48,969	($22,197)	$26,772	13%	10%	$54,615	14%
Dietary	18,516		18,516	13%	33,187		33,187	10%	37,664		37,664	9%	18,028		18,028	9%	11%	36,776	10%
Housekeeping & Laundry	41,153		41,153	29%	13,323		13,323	4%	8,733		8,733	2%	4,340		4,340	2%	3%	8,855	2%
Personal Care	97,408		97,408	68%	126,683		126,683	37%	132,857		132,857	33%	65,633		65,633	32%	20%	133,892	35%
Ancillary	12,065		12,065	8%	15,407		15,407	4%	12,631		12,631	3%	5,143		5,143	3%	3%	10,491	3%
Depreciation	5,045	(5,045)	0	0%	8,152	(8,152)	0	0%	8,303	(8,303)	0	0%	4,145	(4,145)	0	0%	NA	0	0%
Property	55,877		55,877	39%	67,919		67,919	20%	63,701		63,701	16%	33,623		33,623	16%	10%	67,245	18%
Management Fee (5)	0	8,579	8,579	6%	0	20,662	20,662	6%	0	24,704	24,304	6%		12,316	12,316	6%	6%	22,781	6%
Total Expenses	$275,716		$270,671		$340,845		$330,661		$382,100		$362,486		$179,881		$165,855			$338,344	
Expense per Unit			$15,922				$19,451				$18,124				$19,512			$19,903	
EBITDA	($132,735)		($127,690)	-89%	$3,525		$13,709	4%	$22,974		$42,588	11%	$25,385		$39,411	19%	19.35%(2)	$41,340	11%

VALUATION

Method	Rate	Value	Value/Unit
Capitalization Rate	12.0%	$345,000	$20,300
Capitalization Rate	13.0%	$318,000	$18,700
Effective Gross Income Multipliers	1.35	$513,000	$30,200

Notes
(1) Average based on "Assisted Living Development Cost Survey", 1997, Capital Research Group.
(2) Information based on "The State of Seniors Housing 1995, Americans Senior Housing Assoc. and Coopers & Lybrand LLP."
Range represents Lower Quartile to Upper Quartile.
(3) Base year revenue/unit/year is based on actual December 1996 average revenue per resident.
(4) Employees' benefits were allocated to various expense categories based on averages from "Assisted Living Development Cost Survey", 1997.
(5) ORP allocates properties 6% of EGI for corporate overhead, including accounting and legal fees. These charges have been recast from G&A to management fees.
Salaries and benefits relating to the marketing department have been eliminated.

Exhibit 1, Page 7

29

Wilkinson Woods
Adjusted Historical Financials

	1996	Adjustments	Adjusted 1996	% Rev	Six months ended 6/97	Adjustments	Adj 6/97	% Rev	Ntnl Avg(1)	Base Year (2)	% Rev	Stabilized Year(2)	% Rev
# of Units	43				43					43		43	
Revenue/Unit/Year	$1,877				$8,728				$14.3k-23.2k(3)	$14,796 (4)		$24,564 (4)	
Occupancy %	65%				81%					81%		90%	
GROSS POT. INCOME										$636,228		$1,056,240	
VACANCY RESERVE										(118,338)		(105,624)	
EFFECTIVE GROSS INCOME	$80,714		$80,714		$187,648		$187,648			$517,890		$950,616	
EXPENSES (5)													
G&A (6)	$42,141	($16,155)	$25,986	32%	$125,050	($21,140)	$103,909	55%	10%	$211,975	41%	$211,975	22%
Dietary	3,915		3,915	5%	15,039		15,039	8%	11%	30,680	6%	30,680	3%
Housekeeping & Laundry	5,588		5,588	7%	13,125		13,125	7%	3%	26,774	5%	26,774	3%
Personal Care	41,936		41,936	52%	76,585		76,585	41%	20%	156,234	30%	156,234	16%
Ancillary	2,928		2,928	4%	9,974		9,974	5%	3%	20,347	4%	20,347	2%
Depreciation	11,898	(11,898)	0	0%	661	(661)	0	0%	NA	0	0%	0	0%
Property (7)	63,208		63,208	78%	164,269	(14,909)	149,360	80%	10%	304,695	59%	304,695	32%
Management Fee (6)	0	4,843	4,843	6%	0	11,259	11,259	6%	6%	31,073	6%	57,037	6%
Total Expenses	$171,615		$148,405		$404,703		$379,252			$781,779		$807,743	
Expense per Unit			$3,451				$17,640			$18,181		$18,785	
EBITDA	($90,901)		($67,691)	-84%	($217,055)		($191,604)	-102%	197%-355%(3)	($263,889)	-51%	$142,873	15%

VALUATION-Base Year

Method	Rate	Business Value	Real Estate Value(9)		Security Deposit (8)		Total Value	Value/Unit
Capitalization Rate	10.5%	NA	$1,943,000		$500,000		$2,443,000	$56,814
Capitalization Rate	11.5%	NA	$1,774,000		$500,000		$2,274,000	$52,884
Effective Gross Income Multipliers	1.35				$500,000		$1,199,000	$27,884

VALUATION-Stabilized Year

Method	Rate	Business Value (9)	Real Estate Value (9)			Total Value	Value/Unit
Capitalization Rate	10.5%	$1,361,000	$1,943,000			$3,304,000	$76,837
Capitalization Rate	11.5%	$1,242,000	$1,774,000			$3,016,000	$70,140
Effective Gross Income Multipliers	1.35					$1,283,000	$29,837

Notes

(1) Average based on "Assisted Living Development Cost Survey", 1997, Capital Research Group.
(2) Stabilized Year represents full occupancy at the market rental rate. Base year represents value "as is".
(3) Information based on "The State of Seniors Housing, 1995, Americans Senior Housing Assoc. and Coopers & Lybrand LLP.
    Range represents Lower Quartile to Upper Quartile.
(4) Base year revenue/unit/year is based on actual July 1996 average revenue per resident.
(5) Employees' benefits were allocated to various expense categories based on averages from "Assisted Living Development Cost Survey", 1997.
(6) ORP allocates properties 6% of EGI for corporate overhead, including accounting and legal fees. These charges have been recast from G&A to management fees.
    Salaries and benefits relating to the marketing department have been eliminated.
(7) The property is owned and leased to ORP in a non arm's-length transaction. Property expense has been recast to provide for a 12% return on fair market value of real estate.
    Fair market value of the real estate improvements was based on information from the tax assessors' office. The annual lease rate for this property was estimated at $203,988.
(8) Security deposits of approximately $500,000 are held by ORP for tenants with below market rents. It is assumed that as new tenants are brought to market rates,
    these large security deposits will be returned to departing tenants. If ORP were to sell the property "as is", the value was derived from the income stream and not from
    the balance sheet. Therefore ORP would retain the security deposits in an "as is" sale.
(9) Real estate value was derived from capitalizing the property's estimated annual lease rate of $55,104 at the cap rate shown.

Exhibit 1, Page 8

NOTES

BED SELLS (WAIVER) VERSUS 1/12 CONTRACT (BLOCK GRANTS)

Background

In the early 1990s, Home and Community Based Services (HCBS) Medicaid Waiver was in full swing in most states. Wisconsin took full advantage of the federal match for services for developmentally disabled (DD) individuals who were able to access services in the community. In some cases, the match approached seventy cents per dollar spent on the cost of care. This enticed states to make a seismic shift in the redesign of its delivery system to capture those federal dollars. Starting from zero in 1984, the number of HCBS waiver participants in Wisconsin had grown to almost 20,000 individuals by 2010. To be sure, waiver spending per participant has fallen in recent years from a high of $55,000 per person in 2003 to $31,000 in 2009, largely a result of a larger caseload with less intensive needs on average. But HCBS waiver dollars has become the main resource for DD services provided in the community.

HIL started to enter "waiver world" by 1990. This new system would fundamentally change the business model of HIL. Before the advent of HCBS, services for DD individuals were usually administered by "block grants." This meant that money was pooled into "blocks" of money by service type (e.g., mental illness, alcohol and drug abuse, developmental disabilities) based on permitted uses. If there were a federal match, that match would be combined with state and county funds to create the pool of money (the block) to be distributed to community-based organizations according to plans developed by local planning councils, typically updated every two years. Those planning council recommendations provided the market intelligence that agencies like HIL would rely on to determine where the money would flow for new programs. Each of the Human Services departments in 72 Wisconsin counties would distribute the funding dollars.

HCBS: Opportunity or Disaster?

Before waiver world, the contract of choice was the one-twelfth (1/12) contract whereby a county would enter an agreement with an agency (e.g., HIL) to operate a program that satisfied the criteria set by each county's planning council. Marketing staff and management would scour the recommendations and request for proposals (RFPs) from the county planning councils that laid down the road maps for where funding would go. Providers would then pitch the county officials for this new business, as they were responsible for the execution of the plans and distribution of the funds through annual contracts with provider agencies. Counties would purchase a program—for example, an eight-bed group home or a community support program for X amount of hours of service per year—and the agency would bill monthly for its services. This was an excellent model for HIL because it could easily predict its monthly revenue under the annual contract, and the risk of vacancy fell upon the county, not the company, absent extreme circumstances.

HCBS waiver would alter the way HIL had to do business. New contracts were becoming harder to come by, as counties were now taking an interest in waiver because of the federal match. The leveraging effect of the match allowed state and county dollars to serve a broader set of needs in the market. But a distinguishing feature of HCBS waiver was that it had very strict rules on payments. A day of care was paid for only when actually provided. This sounds reasonable on the surface, but it raises serious operational issues. What if a client is hospitalized and you must hold the bed indefinitely for his/her return? Generally you would not get paid by waiver dollars. What if you were launching a new start-up? The agency would have to absorb the start-up losses (see the start-up graph on page 75 of the text).

HIL faced a strategic decision:

1. Should it change its business model and implement a bed sell model targeting waiver dollars for individuals with disabilities? If it did, it would have to absorb a significant start-up investment for each program. HCBS revenue would only be realized after services began to be provided. HIL would have to absorb all start-up costs in hopes that a program would become successful and offset over time the start-up losses incurred. What if the start-up was slower than planned? What if the expected revenue never materialized? What if another provider undercut HIL's rate?

2. Alternatively, should HIL continue to solicit new business from the old block grant program, leaving the risk of HCBS waiver to other providers? This would minimize start-up losses and provide for safer start-ups. But, the number of opportunities under this model appeared to be dwindling.

Discussion question: How would the start-up graph 9-2 on page 75 of the text change given a 1/12 contract and the same expenses? Please explain.

Discussion question: Draw a new start-up graph for a 1/12 contract start-up and explain what happens to the start-up losses in the shaded area.

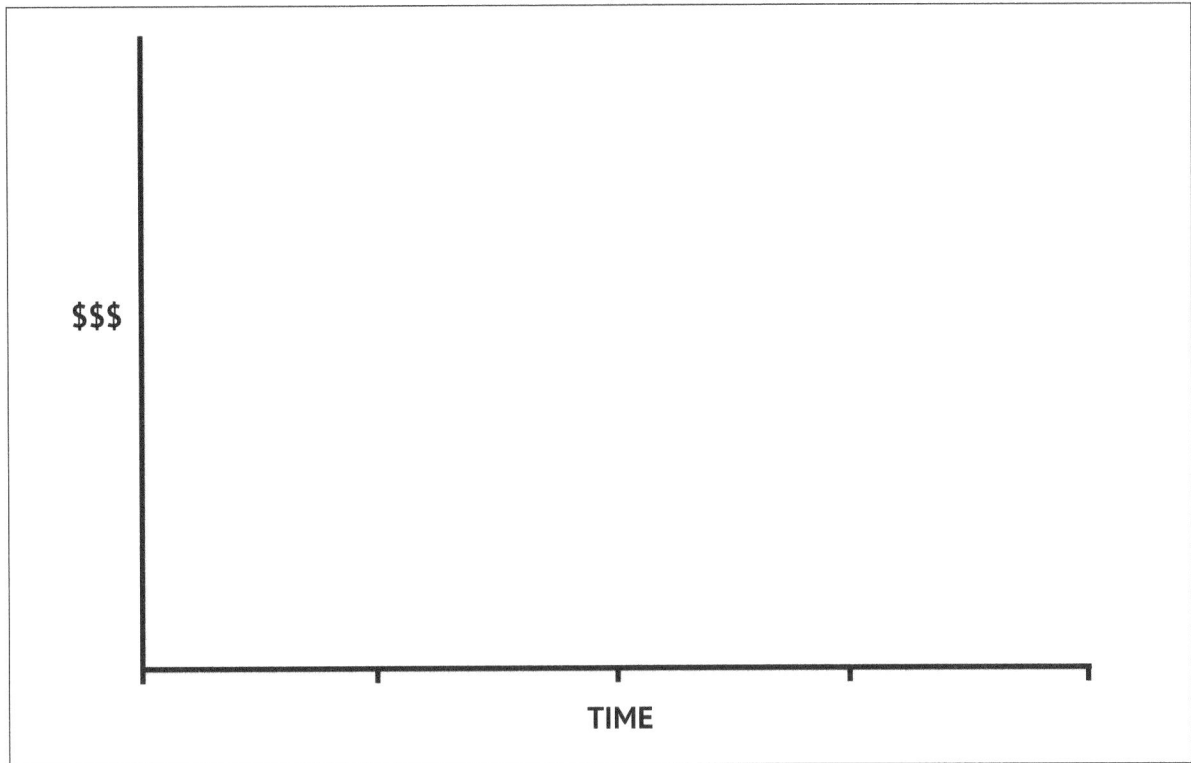

Start-Up Graph: Include Start-Up Loss, Fixed Costs, Variable Costs, Revenue, Breakeven Point, and Operating Profit

Discussion question: Where would the capital come from to do new waiver start-ups (bed sells)?

_____

_____

_____

_____

_____

Discussion question: Which model, waiver or 1/12 contract, do you think had more potential for growth?

_____

_____

_____

_____

Discussion question: What do you think are the five most important questions for management to ask before determining a course of action in this area?

_____

_____

_____

_____

_____

_____

_____

_____

_____

NOTES

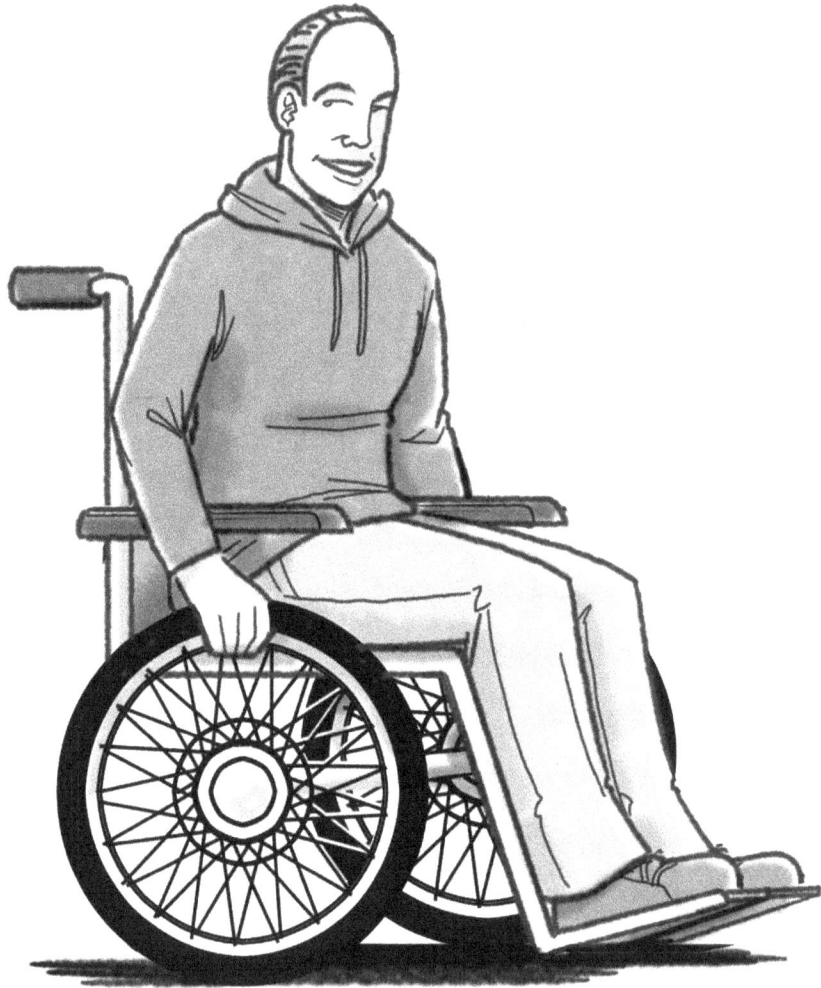

HOMES FOR INDEPENDENT LIVING (HIL)

Case Overview

The Environment. In the second half of the 20th century, it became increasingly clear that congregate care models for people with developmental disabilities or mental illness were failing. Models of treatment emerged that encouraged integration with the family and the community. The mode of care turned to social welfare and not medical needs. These new models promoted "inclusion" in the community and focused on creating accommodations that could enable a person with a particular disability or limitation to thrive. Advocacy organizations, parent groups, and disabilities associations—emboldened after the civil rights movements of the 1960s—began to acquire a louder voice and to insert themselves into the public discourse on disabilities.

Also taking root was the deinstitutionalization movement, which directed treatment and care to smaller community-based alternatives and family supports. Political activism escalated, focusing on the right to treatment for people who were, or could become at risk of becoming, institutionalized. This was fueled by the success of various lawsuits and legislative actions. Landmark legislation was enacted, such as Section 504 of the Rehabilitation Act (1973), which prohibited entities receiving federal funding from discriminating against people with disabilities, and the Americans with Disabilities Act (1990), which barred discrimination against people with disabilities in employment, public service, and public accommodations. There was no turning back to the institutional model favored in the first half of the 20th century.

The move to deinstitutionalize people with disabilities was separate and apart from the trend toward privatization of the delivery system. As you will see in this case, state and federal authorities continued to exert influence and control through mandates (many unfunded), rate controls, and other constraints that led to a "semi-privatization" of service delivery. This reality created challenges for human services organizations. If not navigated properly, the pull from government authorities to prevent the complete privatization of the delivery system could quickly doom an otherwise solid company.

The Purchase of HIL. Oconomowoc Residential Programs, Inc. (ORP) purchased Homes for Independent Living (HIL) in October 1984, a time when institutional downsizings and closures were accelerating. The new emphasis was on supported community living for individuals with intellectual disabilities and mental illness, either through Medicaid Home and Community-Based Waiver Services (HCBS) or community block grants. At the time of purchase, HIL had eight community-based programs in small residential settings in local communities in southeastern Wisconsin. All of its revenue was funded from either mental health block grants distributed by local counties or through "state line item" distributed through counties or directly from the State of Wisconsin. HIL began its journey toward becoming a relevant provider of quality human services in the state of Wisconsin.

The Mental Health Market. In general, the settings and responsibility of care for reform in the mental health movement evolved from the asylum (1800s), to mental hospitals (1900–1950), to community health centers (1950–1975), to community supports (1975 to today). The focus of care shifted from humane "restorative" treatments (1800s), to prevention and scientific treatments (1900–1950), to deinstitutionalization and social integration (1950–1975), and finally to treating mental health as a social welfare problem (1975 to present). With deinstitutionalization, mentally ill people flooded the streets, but there was no adequate funding in place to address the "needs of the streets"—ground zero in the campaign. The mentally ill became homeless, were thrown in jail, or engaged in excessive self-medicating use of drugs and alcohol—an unintended and problematic consequence of a movement launched with the best of intentions.

The final "hand washing" of responsibility by the federal government was marked by the enactment of the Omnibus Budget Reconciliation Act of 1981. The Reagan administration promoted this law as a way to reduce domestic spending. But the act effectively ended federal funding of community treatment for the mentally ill and shifted the burden almost entirely to state governments.

From 1975 to 1995, local groups in Wisconsin sought to establish community support programs for the mentally ill that included: (1) community-based residential care, (2) supervised apartments, (3) vocational training, (4) emergency care, and (5) responsible case management. Although HIL had experienced success in serving clients with mental health issues, the drop in funding cut short this success, and potential clients succumbed to homelessness, the corrections systems, or alcohol and other drug abuse (AODA). The percentage of mental illness revenue to total revenue for HIL declined each year from 1995 to 2010 and finally became an insignificant percentage, as the developmental disabilities (DD) waiver population of clients continued to climb. It was clear that HIL's future prosperity would depend on Medicaid Waiver business and not the mental health block grant program.

Home and Community-Based Services (HCBS) Medicaid Waiver. Medicaid funds are the main source of support for individuals with DD. These funds provide for the care of almost a half a million individuals in the United States. The passage of the ICF/MR law (Medicaid Title XIX – 1971) enabled states to secure federal matching funds for public institutions, private institutions, nursing facilities, group homes, and intermediate care facilities (ICFs) if the care satisfied minimum federal standards for treatment and space (see page 9 in the text). After its passage, this federal initiative triggered a massive change in the way the human services delivery system operated for individuals with DD. It triggered progress towards the twin goals of enhancing the quality of care for those institutionalized and deinstitutionalizing those who could prosper in a community setting.

Further progress occurred when Congress first authorized the HCBS waiver in 1981. This effected a radical change in the service delivery system. The waiver contemplated a wide range of service delivery types for DD populations that would be authorized under state-by-state "waiver plans" (plans that sought permission to waive strict Medicaid rules). Each state submitted such plans to the U.S. Center for Medicaid Services for review, potential modification, and approval. Wisconsin's plan—modified a number of times over the years—includes Medicaid Waiver funding for case management, assistive technologies, homemaker assistance, home health, personal cares, residential services, day programs, respite care, transportation services, supported employment, home modifications, and various therapies.

Waiver was a game changer for individuals with DD and for HIL. With the decline of the mental health market, HIL rested its plans for future growth on the DD Medicaid Waiver. From the mid-1990s on, HIL increased its revenue by leaps and bounds as state centers downsized, nursing homes discharged DD residents, and children (who were becoming adults) were diverted to waiver. Also fueling the expansion was the Supreme Court's Olmstead decision (see page 10 in the text).

In the days of waiver world, each of 72 Wisconsin counties tailored its human services delivery system to meet its unique requirements. Counties set up planning councils that would assess the needs in that area. Depending on its population, a county typically created a planning council for each segment of human services, such as mental health, DD, AODA, and physical disabilities. These councils would assess and determine the priorities for the spending of human services county budgets. Providers worked closely with county human services departments to match their needs with provider services and capabilities, usually through a request for proposal (RFP) process but sometimes through organic and word-of-mouth growth of programs already under contract. Counties had their fingers on the "pulse" of their community of individuals with disabilities. Often case managers knew by name those who were on their case loads and had known the individuals and families for many years. This tended to lead to effective, appropriate, person-centered service delivery at low cost. But the system created concern among state officials, who were disturbed by the variety of rates and programs, and by the state's lack of control over delivery of funding.

The Advent of Family Care. The Wisconsin Department of Human Services (DHS) was not happy with a system where 72 separate counties planned and implemented the public policy surrounding needs of individuals with DD. Nor was it happy with the way the counties managed the funding and administration of these programs. Although waiver world offered significant funding for states to care for people with disabilities, just how to distribute and control this influx of federal match dollars became a topic for debate.

In 1995, the state launched "Long-Term Care Redesign" to address the needs of: (1) the aging and those with chronic conditions, (2) individuals with DD, and (3) individuals with physical disabilities. Mental health and AODA services were not included in the proposed system redesign.

In 1999, Governor Thompson included the Family Care proposal in his 1999–2001 budget requests. It passed both houses of the legislature. Pilots were launched in several counties, and the move to Family Care began. In 2006, Governor Doyle announced plans to expand Family Care statewide with a goal of eliminating waiting lists for community-based long-term care programs within five years.

The exact reasons behind the switch from local county delivery to managed care under state supervision are open to debate. After several years of study, Wisconsin DHS determined that there were serious flaws with the way the state was delivering long-term care. They asserted that people with disabilities, older people, and their families were saying that the system "often didn't make good sense" and did not meet their needs. No one was happy with the long waiting lists for services in many counties. The DHS list of complaints about the county system was lengthy: (1) the system was not dependable, (2) it cost too much, (3) it was not responsive to individual needs, (4) it was too complicated, and (5) accountability was fragmented.

The state's analysis purported to show that it could be far more efficient and serve more people for the same amount of money under a managed care system. The goals of the DHS redesign were:

(1) to become more responsive and give people better choices in their care; (2) to become more reliable, fair, and consistent across the state with respect to level of care; (3) to be more transparent and less complex by offering one-stop shopping through the Aging and Disability Resource Centers (ADRCs); (4) to promote accountability; and (5) probably most important, to become more affordable now and into the future (i.e., austerity).

The Economic Recession of 2008. Shortly after Governor Doyle's 2006 announcement of plans to implement Family Care statewide, the United States economy started to sputter. By 2007, ominous storm clouds were building, and the country faced a serious recession the next year. Normally, human services budgets lag the general economy by one or two years due to budget cycles, but in this case the effects were felt DURING the current budget cycle—a very bad sign. The recession hit during the middle of the Family Care rollout, and tax collections plummeted. This exacerbated the wide-reaching effects of the transition to the new model. As one rate cut after another was announced, HIL and other providers immediately began to feel the effects of two of the drivers of the transition to managed care; the desire for austerity and centralized control.

The underlying push for austerity surfaced in several areas. First was in client assessments. The ADRCs were set up to provide an arm's-length professional assessment of individual need to determine a level of care (need) within the managed care system. The state intentionally fashioned the ADRCs to be separate and distinct from the Managed Care Organizations (MCOs) to ensure the integrity of the delivery system. Yet there was a perception that the austerity goals that were inherent in the system design would pressure the MCOs to offer more restrictive assessments of client needs.

A second sign of austerity was the rates negotiated between the MCOs and the providers. The MCOs were reimbursed on a capitation rate—that is, they received a flat amount from the state to serve the needs of each person in their care. They were highly motivated to cut rates to providers, since this helped their bottom line. So rate cuts became a standard operating procedure.

The Family Care Rate Setting Model. One of the aspects of the county system that was most irksome to DHS was the perceived lack of uniformity in rates. During 2009 and 2010, DHS attempted to implement a rate setting methodology that would create uniformity in the rate setting process. The goal was for the state to set the rates that the MCOs would pay providers for designated services. DHS wanted to control the assessment process though the ADRCs and to control the rate setting process through an algorithm designed by certain University of Wisconsin professors under the supervision of the DHS. It was an attempt to put a round peg into a square hole.

After numerous failed attempts to have the algorithm reflect the reality on the ground, the model was shelved, though it may appear later. That failure did not deter the MCOs from attempting to design other rate setting methodologies of their own and implementing them through various techniques. After repeated attempts to cut rates from 2009 through 2012, the jury remains out on the question of whether a robust provider network can survive the austerity measures of the MCOs. So far, DHS has looked the other way on these rate setting attempts by the MCOs but continues to put an emphasis on austerity by placing financial constraints on them through strict oversight of the capitation rates.

Medicaid and Politics, 2010 Version. For the most part, Medicaid is the sole source of long-term care and medical funding for the long-term care delivery system in this country. It provides for the needs of a disabilities community that numbers almost a half million people. Yet since its inception in the 1960s, Medicaid has been a target of political controversy. Some do not think the country needs the social safety net represented by Medicaid. Others believe it is an essential part of a humane "great society."

Whatever the political discussion, for its current business, HIL is highly dependent on Medicaid and on the health of the federal Medicaid budget. The reality at this time is "how Medicaid goes, HIL goes." While efforts to diversify revenue are ongoing, this remains true in 2013 as HIL currently receives about 80% of its revenue from Medicaid.

What the future holds for Medicaid budgets is anybody's guess.

1. It is possible the decision will be made to convert Medicaid to a block grant program, transferring control to the individual states and effectively giving each state a "flavor of the day" approach to the delivery system, which would have minimal federal oversight and which could change from election to election.

2. It is possible austerity measures will exact their toll on Medicaid budgets in the future, effectively "starving the beast" of the long-term care system.

3. It is possible that Medicaid could be rolled back altogether in whole or in part, turning the clock back to an earlier time when the ability of individuals with disabilities to enforce rights and to receive services was sharply curtailed.

The Effects of Managed Care on HIL. The implementation of the managed care model of Family Care has been a game changer for HIL and has significantly affected HIL's financial results. It has caused general unrest among staff and has been disruptive and upsetting to clients and their families. It also triggered significant HIL introspection as to its structure, its faith in government authorities, its faith in elected officials, the need for diversification of revenue, the implications on the quality of life for its clients, and its view of the future. More than once, questions have been asked such as "Do we have the ability to operate successfully in this new managed care world?" or "Is this the new normal?"

We will look at these effects in depth later in the case. We will analyze what HIL has done in the face of all this change, and what strategies the company has put in place to continue to carry out its mission. We will also perform some self-examination regarding whether the chosen strategies are the ones most likely to achieve continued success.

Analysis By Chapter

Chapter 3 – Public Policy. Medicaid is a national program but is administered by the individual states. The "Feds" control the agenda by linking the federal Medicaid match to rules that must be followed for states to receive the match. A state can request a waiver of the federal Medicaid rules to use the federal match to implement waiver services. The HCBS waiver, in theory, assists individuals with disabilities to live in the "least restrictive or most normalized setting possible." The goal of the waiver is to ensure that those in need avoid more restrictive institutional care.

Therein lays both the problem and the potential solution for HIL and the clients it serves. HIL managers believe the state is interpreting its approved waiver plan in a way that heightens the chances that its constituents will be forced to move to more restrictive environments. They also believe their residents will suffer needlessly or sacrifice their rights of care under the federal Medicaid program, as the state imposes austerity measures that may violate federal law. Finally, they believe the solution is to demand that the state follow federal Medicaid law.

State government in Wisconsin includes the legislative branch (which approved the switch to managed care), the executive agency DHS (which creates administrative rules and interprets and executes statutory requirements), and the judicial branch (which enforces rights guaranteed under law). Many providers believe that DHS (the executive branch) is implementing the new managed care system in a way that is violating the law, and provider agencies and advocacy groups have filed a complaint in United States District Court seeking a legal resolution to assist it in planning operations in the future.

The core of the plaintiffs' argument is that DHS and several named MCOs have carried out the managed care system in a way that systematically discriminates against those individuals that have the most severe support needs. The motivation is that these are the higher-cost clients, so more savings can be generated by targeting rate cuts to this population. To be specific, the lawsuit claims the Wisconsin DHS has violated the following:

1. *The Rehabilitation Act (page 9, point 6 in the text) in four areas:*
   a. *Discrimination on the basis of disability*
   b. *Most integrated setting*
   c. *Program access and methods of administration*
   d. *Facility access and methods of administration*

2. *Title II of the Americans with Disabilities Act (page 10, point 8 in the text) in four areas:*
   a. *Discrimination on the basis of disability*
   b. *Most integrated setting*
   c. *Program access and methods of administration*
   d. *Facility access and methods of administration*

3. Title III of the Americans with Disabilities Act in four areas:
   a. Discrimination on the basis of disability
   b. Most integrated setting
   c. Program access and methods of administration
   d. Facility access and methods of administration

4. The United States Constitution:
   a. First Amendment Right of Association
   b. Fourteenth Amendment Due Process

The coalition seeks: (1) class action status; (2) a preliminary injunction to restore rates to January 1, 2012, levels; (3) declaratory judgment that DHS and several named MCOs are violating the previously described; (4) a permanent injunction until a reasonable rate setting methodology can be put in place; and (5) legal fees.

In the view of HIL management, successful court intervention would significantly increase the probability that HIL can survive and flourish in the future. Absent court intervention, the adult human services delivery system in Wisconsin will continue to take significant blows that could jeopardize its very existence.

Discussion question: Do you think it is a good or bad idea for provider agencies to be involved in this lawsuit? Why?

_____

_____

_____

_____

_____

_____

Discussion question: In what ways could DHS or the MCOs retaliate against the parties in the lawsuit?

_____

_____

_____

_____

_____

_____

_____

Discussion question: Can you think of more effective ways to get the changes needed in the delivery system other than litigating (hint: think of the three branches of government)? What are the pros and cons of pursuing alternative approaches?

Chapter 8 – Licensing and Rule-Making Authority. HIL was experiencing both rate cuts for particular clients and reductions in services. Rate cuts can be particularly devastating to a company that operates small community-based living arrangements. They have ranged from as little as a few percentage points to as much as 50%. To complicate matters, the rate cuts were announced randomly, sometimes as often as twice a year. Exhibit #1 illustrates the effects of rate cuts of 5%, 15%, and 25% on a typical eight-bed Community Living Arrangement (CLA), assuming the days of care remains constant. It should be apparent that rate cuts jeopardize the long-term sustainability of the program.

Going through a prolonged period of sustained rate cuts is a humbling experience. What was going to happen to the HIL mission? How could management shelter the effects of the MCO rate cuts from the clients? How would the state react to the adaptation HIL was forced to make in its operations in response to the rate cuts, including some discharges of clients who could no longer be served? At what point must a decision be made to close a program? Questions that are never on the radar screen when funding is bountiful become paramount concerns when the environment shifts. What was amazing was that the MCOs appeared to believe they could implement significant, even draconian, rate reductions with virtually no ramifications for programs, clients, or families.

For HIL, the epiphany struck in 2011 when the company was struggling with yet another round of rate cuts and its effects on operations. Was it now the case that to continue to operate, HIL would be forced to host programs in unlicensed settings? Would that become the new normal? If they reinvented the business from the ground up, could they devise a way to serve HCBS clients within the new rates that were unavoidable in the new austerity environment?

HIL began to think it just might work. But how would the MCOs, state licensing officials, guardians, and clients react? And would all parties would be better off with this new model of service delivery? Licensing costs money—lots of it—for the required staffing patterns, mandatory staff training, licensee responsibilities of treatment and care, resident rights, physical environment, and safety. The jury is out, but this is one of the paths HIL has selected. To the extent it succeeds, HIL will be able to continue to serve its clients. If the path is blocked and there are no rate increases, HIL will have to discharge clients, who will then turn to other (cheaper) providers or move to less appropriate settings.

Discussion question: What are the pros and cons of licensed vs. unlicensed programs?

_____

_____

_____

_____

_____

Discussion question: What would you do if licensing blocks the plan?

_____

_____

_____

_____

Discussion question: Would you notify licensing of your intentions before implementation? Why or why not?

_____

_____

_____

_____

Discussion question: Do you think that migrating HIL licensed programs to unlicensed settings for HCBS violates federal law, state law, or municipal law?

_____

_____

_____

_____

_____

Discussion question: Do you think these violations could be trumped by the "reasonable accommodation" clause of ADA?

Chapter 11 – Closing a Program. No human services provider wants to close a program, but sometimes its best efforts fail and it is best to do so. Closing for financial reasons due to rate or service cuts, dictated by those who have no direct contact with or understanding of the needs of the people served, is especially troubling. To put it simply, any relocation puts residents with disabilities at risk. Sometimes the risks are emotional, causing breakdowns or other severe emotional reactions. Sometimes the risks are medical, resulting in stress-related conditions or even death.

Because of the changes in managed care, HIL was forced to discharge almost 75 residents from its care over several years. HIL managers understand they cannot knowingly subsidize a funding system that is inherently flawed by continuing to serve clients at rates below the cost of serving them. If HIL were to continue under these circumstances, the effects would spill over into other parts of its business and prevent the company from accumulating the investment capital it needs for new programs.

Review Exhibit #1 and consider some of the expenses you could cut in order to make margin. Reductions in staff clearly have a limit. Hourly wage cuts are generally not possible. Lowering the rent, turning down the heat, eating less, eliminating a vehicle, or reducing overtime might be possible and offer some temporary relief, but even these measures yield minimal savings in the face of rate cuts of up to 40%.

After trying all other scenarios and alternatives, HIL was forced to close a CLA occasionally. In that case, the first task for management was to minimize closing costs. Review 11-1: Closure Graph on page 101 of the text and Exhibit #2 to get a visual picture of the factors to consider when closing a program. When can fixed costs be eliminated, variable costs lowered, or revenue extended? You can see from the graph that time is money.

Once it had developed its plan of closure, HIL carried out a careful communications plan, taking into account the effects on clients, families, guardians, and employees. Most importantly, from the onset, management stressed the need for complete, open, and honest communication with all affected parties about all aspects of the program closure. Even if the outcome is not favorable, people can process bad news much more effectively if they believe the company has treated them with respect, honesty, and fairness.

Ironically, when it became apparent that HIL was not just making an empty threat to close a program as a negotiating tactic, the MCO would reverse course and restore previously announced rates or service arrangements. Families can be very powerful advocates when decisions are made that are not in the best interests of their loved ones. This trend was more noticeable in situations where programming alternatives were hard to find and the case managers were forced to scramble to locate acceptable settings.

To be clear, rates cuts or service cuts were done to benefit the payer, not the provider or the client, so when the benefit ceases to accrue for payers like the MCOs, positions can magically and quickly change. HIL thought through these situations strategically, pushing back, and working with advocacy groups or guardians in an attempt to minimize the effects on its clients and on operations, sometimes with great success. HIL also strove for a "meeting of the minds" to preserve the MCO customer relationship for the future.

Discussion question: In what circumstances might HIL continue to run a program that generates a negative contribution margin?

Discussion question: In what circumstances might HIL continue to serve clients whose rates are insufficient to pay for their cost of care?

Discussion question: To what extent should HIL try to shield the clients, HIL staff, or guardians from the effects of MCO rate cuts?

Chapter 14 – Financial Management. With the advent of the managed care model for Medicaid HCBS, it was obvious that HIL would have no choice but to diversify its revenue base and service offerings. Management undertook a diversification and portfolio analysis of its marketplace options in 2010 and 2011. There were two problems:

1. A small group of customers accounted for 100% of its revenue. In the days before managed care, HIL had at least 72 different actual or potential county customers in Wisconsin, and hundreds more if further divided into disability specialty areas within the counties. Now HIL was facing a total customer count of about 10, with 80% of its revenue coming from three MCOs. Meanwhile, the state was attempting to centralize the rate setting function after already having centralized the assessment models and process. This was causing HIL's business risk to climb to unacceptable levels.

2. In addition to customer risk, HIL was concerned that the bulk of its revenue flowed from one type of HCBS waiver service. Management was concerned about licensing, unfunded mandates, regulators, and an increasingly adversarial relationship between the provider network and the state.

When it was all said and done, HIL staff determined that it employed too few license types, was too dependent on a few customers, and focused on only one type of market (Medicaid Waiver). Because of this, the company needed to diversify service offerings and expand its customer base. An example of diversification is the current emphasis on exploring and securing county-funded mental health service contracts funded through community block grants. However, HIL officials have determined that this is only a partial solution to the MCO situation and is exploring other service lines in the hope that it can apply its significant intellectual property to serve other populations. These efforts could pay off with program successes that will supplement or replace disappearing HCBS services.

Discussion question: Why do you think HIL waited so long to diversify its service line?

Discussion question: Considering the core competencies of HIL, can you think of adjacent service lines that HIL might successfully penetrate?

Discussion question: Do you think it was the job of the finance department to discover and highlight the risks the conversion to managed care would present for the company? If not, who should have been on this—the CEO, HIL staff, and/or others?

Chapter 16 – Sales, Marketing, and Generating Revenue. With significant rate and service cuts, HIL faced the dilemma that its brand identity—as the higher cost, high-quality provider for clients who are difficult to serve—could be derailed. HIL was aware that rate cuts could compromise its mission and that good business discipline was critical, though this might require painful decisions.

Management viewed pending discharges through the lens of the Lifetime Sales Model (see page 179 in the text). They realized results of a discharge could be harmful to the organization. The average HIL daily rate for a residential client in 2012 was about $240 per day. The loss of that adult client 10 years early amounted to a loss of $876,000 ($240 cost per day × 365 days in a year × 10 years)! When HIL managers thought about a discharge in that light, the impact of the move became real and prompted them to consider many innovative options before deciding on discharge or program closure.

Because of the consolidation of the HCBS waiver into the managed care model, HIL's new MCO customers could be divided into categories (see page 182 of the text). Some were "strategic" in the sense that they were in the sweet spot of HIL's core competence. These were customers HIL was likely to retain because there were few alternative providers who could offer suitable settings. Other customers were "significant," because they may have provided a substantial revenue stream, but they appeared to be harder to keep because other providers were capable of serving those clients or because "profitability" was elusive.

Yet HIL looked systematically and painstakingly at every program and every client to see if there were possible changes within its control that could reset the profitability landscape. This could include changes in program census capacity, pricing, service mix, bundling of services, or other innovative approaches. An orderly exit from MCO business entirely did not seem realistic due to the magnitude of their coverage area with the State of Wisconsin. Other solutions to profitability had to prevail or HIL was at significant risk. Also, HIL clung to the hope that in the long run, MCOs would need a healthy provider network that could serve the needs of clients in their care, because the individuals were not going anywhere.

Discussion question: What are some of the approaches you could take to avoid discharging a long-term client?

_____

_____

_____

_____

_____

Discussion question: What would you consider to be an MCO "soft spot" when it comes to rate setting and discharges?

_____

_____

_____

_____

Discussion question: What checks and balances exist in the human services delivery system to balance the pricing power of the MCOs?

_____

_____

_____

_____

_____

Chapter 18 – Rate Regulation. Although HIL purports to be a private enterprise, the reality is that its business is driven by the government's efforts to control, define, and manipulate rates and services. Whether this is using the allowable costs and profit caps of the county system, the invalidated assessment methods used to determine appropriate level of care, or the often arbitrary daily rates that the MCOs assign to providers, rate setting methodologies have created challenges that could doom HIL if not navigated properly.

As this goes to print, the arbitrary rate setting and austerity measures of the state are being tested in the court system. The outcome is uncertain, but rate regulation is probably here to stay. The theory supporting rate regulation is that, left to its own devices, the market would enable providers to overcharge for services and cost the taxpayer more money. In addition, during times of recession and budget cuts, austerity measures will lower rates as a way to fit within the money available in state budgets. In other words, rates are not based on need but on budget. It is a giant math problem that starts from the answer and goes backward to plug in the inputs and generate the rate amounts.

The rate setting methods the MCOs are using with HIL are constraining profitable market pricing in ways no different from the examples on page 202 of the text. While it is rarely desirable for a provider to operate in an industry that is subject to rate setting, the problem for HIL is that the industry today does not resemble the industry it flourished in just a few short years ago.

HIL has implemented the following strategies to survive in its new rate setting environment:

1. It has increased the divisor whenever possible to increase revenue in a program (i.e., increase the number of beds and census as a way to reduce the per client program rate).

2. It has attempted to build or keep strong relationships with the MCOs even through the rate setting skirmishes.

3. It has pushed back against insufficient rates and never acceded without objecting.

4. It has appealed rates when possible.

5. It has carefully developed and executed a communication strategy within the "triangle of dysfunction" among the provider, the payer, and the end user to exert pressure on the MCOs.

6. It has worked (and continues working) with advocates and other providers to force legal change within the system.

7. It is applying good business boundaries and only selectively discharging clients or closing programs as a last resort.

Discussion question: What would you do if low rates affected program quality?

_____

_____

_____

_____

_____

Discussion question: What would you do if rate regulation interfered with customer expectations?

_____

_____

_____

_____

_____

_____

_____

_____

Discussion question: What would you do if you became aware a program was in the throws of the "death spiral" (see page 207 of the text)?

_____

_____

_____

_____

_____

_____

_____

_____

HIL EXHIBIT #1

EXHIBIT #1

	Actual Dec-12	Budget Dec-12	Variance	5% Reduction Dec-12	15% Reduction Dec-12	25% Reduction Dec-12
Maximum Census	8.00	N/A		8.00	8.00	8.00
Census	8.00	7.60	(0.40)	8.00	8.00	8.00
Days	2,867.00	2,781.60	(85.40)	2,867.00	2,867.00	2,867.00
Rate	116.26	115.44	(0.83)	110.45	98.82	87.20
Revenue						
Fees	333,328	321,101	12,227	316,662	283,329	249,996
Total Revenue	333,328	321,101	12,227	316,662	283,329	249,996
Salaries & Benefits						
Salaries and Wages	130,376	121,946	(8,430)	130,376	130,376	130,376
Payroll Taxes & Benefits	27,825	29,087	1,262	27,825	27,825	27,825
Total Salaries & Benefits	158,201	151,033	(7,168)	158,201	158,201	158,201
General Expenses						
Staff Training, Recruitment, Benefits	356	883	527	356	356	356
Insurance	4,841	4,647	(194)	4,841	4,841	4,841
Depreciation	1,955	1,984	29	1,955	1,955	1,955
Food & Household Supplies	18,762	18,000	(762)	18,762	18,762	18,762
Building Rent, Utilities, & R.E. Taxes	30,213	28,448	(1,765)	30,213	30,213	30,213
Purchased Services	5,090	5,210	120	5,090	5,090	5,090
Office Supplies & Expenses	3,885	3,735	(150)	3,885	3,885	3,885
License & Fees	-	-	-	-	-	-
Program Expenses	2,066	3,500	1,434	2,066	2,066	2,066
Mileage	1,976	2,275	299	1,976	1,976	1,976
Vehicle Gas & Repairs	4,777	4,200	(577)	4,777	4,777	4,777
Vehicle Leases	171	7,992	7,821	171	171	171
Travel & Lodging	-	-	-	-	-	-
Equipment Expense	494	452	(42)	494	494	494
Miscellaneous Non Allowable	-	-	-	-	-	-
Training Dept Allocation	2,406	2,587	181	2,406	2,406	2,406
Allocate - Maintenance	6,317	7,665	1,348	6,317	6,317	6,317
Adm Fee Expenses	10,641	13,154	2,513	10,641	10,641	10,641
Area Expenses	9,635	9,878	243	9,635	9,635	9,635
Region Expenses	14,656	15,822	1,166	14,656	14,656	14,656
Financing Fee Expense	66	205	139	66	66	66
Management Fee - ODTC	-	-	-	-	-	-
Management Fee - ORP Mgt	27,689	28,150	461	27,689	27,689	27,689
Total General Expenses	145,996	158,787	12,791	145,996	145,996	145,996
Total Expenses	304,197	309,820	5,623	304,197	304,197	304,197
	-	-	-	-	-	-
Contribution Margin	56,886	39,636	17,250	40,220	6,887	(26,446)

Exhibit 1

ORP

HIL EXHIBIT #2

EXHIBIT #2
CLOSING PROGRAM

	Actual 2012	Budget 2012	Variance 2012	Actual Dec-12	Actual Jan-13	Actual Feb-13	Actual Mar-13	Actual Apr-13	Actual May-13	Actual Jun-13	Actual Jul-13	Actual Aug-13	Actual Sep-13	Actual Oct-13	Actual Nov-13
Maximum Census	8.00	N/A		8.00	8.00	8.00	8.00	8.00	8.00	8.00	8.00	8.00	8.00	8.00	8.00
Census	8.00	7.60	(0.40)	8.00	7.00	4.00	0.00	0.00	0.00	0.00	0.00	0.00	0.00	0.00	0.00
Days	2,867.00	2,781.60	(85.40)	242.00	232.00	157.00	75.00								
Rate	116.26	115.44	(0.85)	116.26	116.26	116.26	116.26								
Revenue															
Fees	333,328	321,101	12,227	28,136	26,973	18,253	8,720								
Total Revenue	335,328	321,101	12,227	28,136	26,973	18,255	8,720	-	-	-	-	-	-	-	-
Salaries & Benefits															
Salaries and Wages	130,376	121,946	(8,430)	10,496	10,865	10,865	10,865	-	-	-	-	-	-	-	-
Payroll Taxes & Benefits	27,825	29,087	1,262	2,284	2,319	2,319	2,319	-	-	-	-	-	-	-	-
Total Salaries & Benefits	158,201	151,033	(7,168)	12,780	13,183	13,183	13,183	-	-	-	-	-	-	-	-
General Expenses															
Staff Training, Recruitment, Benefits	356	883	527	12	30	30	30	-	-	-	-	-	-	-	-
Insurance	4,841	4,647	(194)	569	416	416	416	21	21	21	21	21	21	-	-
Depreciation	1,955	1,984	29	163	163	163	163	163	163	163	163	163	163	-	-
Food & Household Supplies	18,762	18,000	(762)	1,277	1,606	1,087	519								
Building Rent, Utilities, & R.E. Taxes	30,213	28,448	(1,765)	2,596	2,581	2,581	2,581	2,336	2,336	2,336	2,336	2,336	2,336	-	-
Purchased Services	5,090	5,210	120	122	424	424	424	212	212	212	212	212	212	-	-
Office Supplies & Expenses	3,885	3,735	(150)	277	323	323	323	284	284						
License & Fees															
Program Expenses	2,066	3,500	1,434	100	172	172	172								
Mileage	1,976	2,275	299	373	165	165	165								
Vehicle Gas & Repairs	4,777	4,200	(577)	376	418	418	418								
Vehicle Leases	171	7,992	7,821												
Travel & Lodging															
Equipment Expense	494	452	(42)		41	41	41	41	41	41	41	41	41	-	-
Miscellaneous Non Allowable															
Training Dept Allocation	2,406	2,587	181	176	195	132	63								
Allocate - Maintenance	6,317	7,665	1,348	453	511	346	165								
Adm Fee Expenses	10,641	13,154	2,513	1,297	861	583	278								
Area Expenses	9,655	9,878	243	708	780	528	252								
Region Expenses	14,656	15,822	1,166	1,123	1,186	803	383								
Financing Fee Expense	66	205	139	9	6	6	6								
Management Fee - ODTC															
Management Fee - ORP Mgt	27,689	28,150	461	2,269	2,241	1,516	724								
Management Fee	27,689	28,150	461	2,269	2,241	1,516	724								
Total General Expenses	145,996	158,787	12,791	11,880	12,116	9,731	7,123	3,058	3,058	2,773	2,773	2,773	2,773	-	-
Total Expenses	304,197	309,820	5,623	24,660	25,300	22,914	20,306	3,058	3,058	2,773	2,773	2,773	2,773	-	-
				(0)	(0)	(0)	0	(0)	(0)	(0)	(0)	(0)	(0)		
Contribution Margin	56,886	39,636	17,250	5,754	3,920	(3,139)	(10,856)	(3,058)	(3,058)	(2,773)	(2,773)	(2,773)	(2,773)	(27,284)	(27,284)
Cumulative Margin				5,754	3,920	781	(10,076)	(13,133)	(16,191)	(18,964)	(21,738)	(24,511)	(27,284)	(27,284)	(27,284)

Exhibit 2

NOTES

INDIANA DEVELOPMENTAL TRAINING CENTER (IDTC)

Case Overview

The Creation. Indiana Developmental Training Center (IDTC) was a residential treatment program serving children and adolescents with a diagnosis of developmental disabilities and emotional disturbances. It opened its first location in Indianapolis, Indiana, in 1997 and launched another location in Lafayette, Indiana, in 2000. IDTC operated secure residential, open residential, and community-based living arrangements, and specialized in providing educational services to both residential and community students. By 2004, its maximum collective operating capacity was 220 children aged 6 to 21 years.

The opportunity for IDTC arose from a sister company, Oconomowoc Developmental Training Center (ODTC, recently renamed Genesee Lake School), which had been in operation since 1975, and from a loosely assembled public policy initiative within the Marion County (Indiana) Juvenile Court. The initiative was to bring Marion County children who were placed in out-of-state facilities back to the state.

In the early 1990s, ODTC specialized in serving children and adolescents who were dually diagnosed with emotional disturbances and developmental disabilities. ODTC had expertise in the treatment of a variety of low incidence syndromes and was developing a specific expertise in serving children and young adults with autism and autism spectrum disorders. ODTC served more than 40 children from the State of Indiana; it held contracts with Indiana County Human Services Departments and the Indiana State Board of Education.

The IDTC opportunity was an outgrowth of the economic downturn in 1990–1991 in Indiana and the rest of the United States, which provided the motivation to keep state dollars within Indiana and Marion County specifically. At the time, the State of Indiana had identified about 7,000 children in need of residential treatment. In addition, it was sending approximately 500 children to out-of-state facilities for non-corrections services.

ODTC officials worked with the Marion County juvenile court and a Marion County consultant to solve the out-of-state placement "problem," as they perceived it. Marion County was the center of a six-county region that encompassed the city of Indianapolis and accounted for at least half of the children placed out of state. In addition, the county assigned the consultant the task of finding additional federal "match" money for an array of services paid by state budget line items or county property taxes.

There was a perception at the time that the State of Indiana was missing out on available federal match dollars. The conventional wisdom was that the state dollars could leverage federal money that would support additional services within the delivery system. This attracted the interest of in-state providers because, theoretically, it could generate more business for them. The reality turned out to be different. While it was true that the additional federal matching funds and the children returning home could have created more business for in-state providers, these were merely steps in a long-term plan to return human services funds to the state's general fund as part of an austerity program.

ODTC officials were approached by officials from the Marion County Juvenile Court to develop a plan to return Indiana children from out-of-state facilities (including those placed at ODTC) to a vacant county-owned 385-bed nursing home and psychiatric facility that had been shuttered by Marion County a few years earlier. In this process, ODTC assisted in the design of a project that ultimately led to a request for proposal (RFP). The state sought providers who would use the Marion County Heath Care Center to operate a program for children who would be returning from other states, including Wisconsin. ODTC was awarded the RFP (see Exhibit #1 – Program Purpose). During the due diligence process after the RFP award, ODTC learned that the Marion County Health Care Center would not be a suitable site for this program. ODTC was back to square one.

Then opportunity struck. At a meeting with juvenile court officials, ODTC learned that a local Charter Psychiatric Hospital, Charter North, was closing in nearby Hamilton County. This location was just five miles from the Marion County line. Though not perfect—because the site was outside the county and lacked education space—it would put the new program squarely within the six-county metro region considered ideal for this project.

ODTC purchased the property in early 1997. The 86-bed program opened for business as Indiana Developmental Training Center, or IDTC, on October 30, 1997, after an extended delay in receiving approvals from the state fire marshal during the licensing process. This delay added hundreds of thousands of dollars in start-up costs due to being "staffed up" during the two months they were waiting for state fire marshall approvals. That was the first of many "Welcome to Indiana!" occurrences.

The Growth Years. Once open, IDTC became a significant regional resource for the "ODTC kind of kid"—shorthand for children with a dual diagnosis of developmental disability and behavioral disorder. By the end of 1998, IDTC was approaching full occupancy, operating 42 secure beds and 44 child caring institution (CCI) beds which are less restrictive. Later it would open an additional 40 group home beds in the surrounding community. Within the first year, ODTC sent most of its 45 Indiana children to IDTC. By opening this IDTC program, ORP would continue to serve the population it lost when those children moved back to Indiana. ODTC responded by further developing its "in-state" business model to replace the business lost to IDTC.

By late 1999, IDTC was consistently at full capacity. It was becoming apparent that it had shaken up the provider network, which responded by increasing the supply of beds in an attempt to defend its market position in the state. Even with the increased supply of beds, IDTC was at a crossroads: should it attempt to accommodate increasing demand by offering community-based alternatives, or should it find a new location for the same type of program in another geographical region in Indiana?

Again, opportunity struck. As luck would have it, the Charter Hospital chain was closing all of its psychiatric residential treatment facility operations nationwide. Four Indiana locations became available: South Bend (64 beds), Lafayette (64 beds), Terre Haute (44 beds), and eventually Indianapolis East (108 beds, which later became Resolute Treatment Center, an IDTC competitor). IDTC officials toured all of the locations except the Indianapolis site and determined that although both the Lafayette and South Bend locations would be suitable options, the Lafayette location and setting was superior. With the availability of these properties, the priority for the community-based approach fell to a distant third. IDTC purchased Charter Lafayette and launched an IDTC operation there in 2000.

Over the next five years, the two IDTCs developed their distinctive "flavors" and cultures. The Lafayette location offered programming attuned to younger, nonverbal, developmentally disabled (DD) boys and older, higher functioning DD girls. The Indianapolis location continued to concentrate on an older (up to 21 years of age) male DD population with serious emotional disturbances. Both programs had private, secure options available. One among only a handful of states, Indiana offered a license type that allowed the locking of a facility in a non-psychiatric setting. This made the IDTCs unique in that children who needed a secure setting could receive appropriate and cost-effective programming, including the important education component, on a long-term basis.

During the 1990s, it became increasingly evident that human services funding for children's treatment programs was going to become scarce. At the same time, courts were strengthening the rights of children and parents under the Individuals with Disabilities Education Act (IDEA). This offered a very viable funding alternative for children who needed extraordinary educational service along with treatment. One distinction between psychiatric facilities, correctional facilities, and residential treatment facilities was that education tended to be a major focus only in residential treatment settings. While the typical stay in a residential care center was about two years, the average length of stay in a psychiatric facility was steadily declining from a maximum of about 90 days to a more typical 3 to 14 days. This rendered an education offering unnecessary. The psychiatric facility "might" perform case coordination with the child's local school district as part of the discharge planning process, but that was usually the extent of it.

Because the availability of quality education services became one of the key factors that distinguished ODTC and IDTC in the marketplace, and because neither building had sufficient educational infrastructure, the next order of business was to invest in state-of-the-art educational facilities in both locations. The cost to the company approached $12 million (about $6 million each). The education edition at the Indianapolis site was completed in early 2005, and the Lafayette school addition was complete in time for the opening of the 2007 school year.

The Harbinger of Change. In 1999, IDTC encountered a situation with rates that turned out to be a forerunner of events to come. At that time, IDTC was free to set its own rate. Any customer enjoyed the choice either to accept the daily IDTC rate or to turn to other providers for services. For the first time, a Marion County juvenile court judge tried to cut a proposed rate increase from 3% to 2%. That turned out to be a shot across the bow. While 1% may not sound like much, inflation was an economic scourge all through the 1970s, 1980s, and 1990s. It eroded the power of the dollar in very real terms for businesses of all types. It was also significant that the same people who actively encouraged the company to set up shop in Indiana were now trying to control rates without proper authority or a defined rate setting process.

For fiscal year 1999, IDTC officials stood firm on the 3% rate increase. IDTC referrals from Marion County promptly slowed and eventually ceased altogether, a direct response to a county directive that case managers were not to make referrals to IDTC because it had no approved rate. It was becoming clear that the relationship with the agency that had persuaded the company to come to

Indiana had soured and IDTC's largest customer was now history. It also became clear that some of the more "cost effective" alternatives chosen by Marion County officials were going to have a negative effect on the children, such as using corrections instead of IDTC.

The loss of its largest customer prompted IDTC to look elsewhere to replace the lost business. Prompted by demand under IDEA, the Indiana State Board of Education (ISBOE) took the place of Marion County as IDTC's largest customer. Other states were also inquiring about IDTC's services, and the future was becoming clear: grow nationally in the education market on the coattails of IDEA, or die a slow and painful death.

In 2004, Indiana elected a new governor. While this may seem like a minor event, it soon became clear that the "elections have consequences" mantra was well founded. One of the governor's new initiatives was to split state human services functions into an adult bureau and a children's bureau. In 2005, the Department of Child Services (DCS) was born. DCS asserted control over children's services that previously rested with local county offices and continued to exercise licensing authority over all agencies providing children's services in the state.

The economic crash of 2008 hit Indiana abruptly, as it did the rest of the country. Jobs vaporized, manufacturing plants closed, and tax collections plummeted. Indiana's governor was a fiscal conservative who had been the budget director for the Bush administration from 2000 to 2004, a very powerful and influential position. A government saying is "never let a good crisis go to waste." The new administration quickly seized the moment to dismantle the old system for children's services and bring in the new.

Human services budgets usually lag general economic conditions by about two years because of biannual budget cycles used by most states. Toll roads were sold, community supports were cut, and state education supports were slashed. For IDTC and similar providers, DCS began to implement a rate setting methodology and other philosophical changes that would: (1) cut provider rates, (2) downsize the use of out-of-home service placements throughout the state, and (3) adjust DCS expenditures downward in relation to decreasing levels of state tax collections.

By 2010, the implementation of a new DCS rate setting model was in full swing. The worry for IDTC was on two levels. First, the DCS census from the Indiana counties represented about 50% of total occupancy. Second, IDTC was concerned that, absent a separate rate setting model, the ISBOE was going to "piggyback" its rate to match the DCS rate. This would account for another 40% of their census being under the new rate regulation, leaving only about 10% of their revenue, the out-of-state placements, within their rate setting control. Fortunately, this did not occur and the ISBOE remained a significant, strategic, and profitable customer.

Control was the key word. DCS had wrested control of placements from the counties, control of the rate negotiations from the counties and the providers, and control of the philosophy of care from the counties, and had consolidated it within essentially one person—the head of DCS. This was done in a way that offered no checks and balances. DCS had also changed its focus from being a human services agency, focusing on the well-being of its constituents, to seeking to maximize the money that could be returned to the general fund of the State of Indiana. It turned out that over $300 million of the DCS budget allocation for the latest biannual budget period was returned unspent, a figure that would have paid for the annual placement of over 2,400 children at IDTC's daily rates or thousands of foster care placements.

Citizens, newspapers, and providers began to voice their displeasure with DCS. This culminated in the filing of a lawsuit in December 2010 by IARRCA, the association in Indiana that represented most of the state's providers of children's services, including the IDTCs. A federal judge granted an order restraining DCS from any more rate cuts until it produced a rate setting methodology that was acceptable under state statute.

The effect of the lawsuit was to chill even further the relationship between DCS and providers. Even though DCS could not cut rates, it continued to operate in a unilateral fashion, cutting referrals and placements to agencies and instituting cost saving measures that many said put the children of Indiana in danger. One of the most unpopular was the centralization of the emergency call center. This very effectively took the local DCS office out the equation when addressing emergency situations within local communities within Indiana. This step could be used to "manage the numbers" (e.g., help with outcomes reporting) and to prevent out-of-home placements, thereby saving DCS money.

As of late 2012, when this case study is being written, DCS has implemented a rate setting methodology and rules acceptable to the court, the lawsuit between DCS and IARRCA has settled, the DCS director has resigned, and a new governor has been elected.

The Closure. In 2009, IDTC began to consider what was previously unthinkable. Would DCS drive IDTC out of business? Would DCS force IDTC to abandon its mission and end its ability to stay open? Would DCS dismantle the delivery system before anyone would intervene? Were programs like those offered by IDTC finished? These sorts of questions can have an insidious effect on staff and stakeholders. Back then, negative news was everywhere. Rate cuts, job losses, philosophy changes—was this the new normal?

The DCS census at IDTC once was as high as 120 children. By mid-2011, it had plummeted to 75. IDTC was completely exposed to DCS because it had not sufficiently diversified its revenue in earlier years when it had the time to do so. DCS was candid about its long-term intent to reduce the number of out-of-home placements from about 2,500 (in 2007) to 500. That raised a strategic question: should IDTC limit DCS census to a particular number at any one time—40, 75, 90, or 110 children—as a way of "forcing" itself to diversify? If referrals from other sources fell short, this tactic would have caused IDTC to forego significant short-term revenue. Perhaps IDTC was in denial as to whether DCS business really could disappear overnight. Did that keep the company from the hard work of successfully developing new out-of-state customers to replace the census numbers lost to the DCS fiasco? We will never know. In hindsight, the thought of limiting DCS admissions seemed too counterintuitive to pursue. How could IDTC not serve a market (and end user) that clearly needed its services? It did not seem right to IDTC managers.

Toward the end of 2011, IDTC management made the decision to close Indianapolis. They did not think the business model was sustainable, given the current environment. It was a decision made with a heavy heart, as IDTC Indianapolis had served almost 800 children in its 15 years of operations. A plan of closure was developed and communicated, and IDTC successfully discharged 75 children to alternative settings by May 25, 2012, the last day of operations. IDTC consolidated operations in its Lafayette program, which remained open as T.C. Harris School and which adopted a strategy of continuing to diversify away from DCS while serving children from ISBOE and other states.

The decision was made somewhat easier because IDTC was presented with a new business opportunity: to use the IDTC Indianapolis facility to open a large program for adults with developmental disabilities and behavior or neurological disorders. That program opened for business on September 11, 2012. It seemed the right option, given the choice of an adult services offering with potential annual revenue in excess of $20 million and a children's program with $12 million in annual revenue.

Analysis By Chapter

Chapter 3 – Public Policy. It is critical that leaders of a human services company understand and track major public policy issues that affect its business. Though it may not have prevented the ultimate outcome of closure, the fact that IDTC was actively involved and aware of the public policy decisions and motivations of DCS, often on a daily basis, definitely helped minimize financial losses during the last four years of IDTC operations.

National public policy think tanks had the ear of DCS and had stated positions that were potentially antithetical to IDTC operations. DCS was free to influence and even dictate legislative policy on the Indiana delivery system, which used federal matching funds, because the federal Health and Human Services agency was silent as to the type of delivery system that Indiana should use to care for the needs of its children. In this case: (1) the legislative branch (the Indiana legislature) authorized the creation of DCS in 2005 but exempted the agency from many administrative review processes and procedures; (2) the executive branch (the governor and DCS political appointee) used the legislative actions to carry out its plans for restructuring the children's delivery system to save money and consolidate control; and (3) ultimately, the judicial branch interfered with the legislative and executive branch plans, as the federal court enjoined any rate decreases pending DCS's creation of a more transparent rate setting methodology and the restructuring of the children's delivery system.

Human services policy is highly sensitive to the political climate ("Elections have consequences"). The IDTC case provides an example of how many forces affected human services policy in Indiana—think tank philosophies, partisan policy, ideology, and "the trifecta," that is, control of the governor's office, the state house, and the state senate by one political party. This muffled voices of dissent and laid the groundwork for massive changes in the human services delivery system to occur very quickly, with little thought or analysis about potential ramifications.

Discussion question: Can you think of an example where a public policy issue has created a programming opportunity for a human services company?

Discussion question: Can you think of a human services business that was not a result of a public policy initiative?

Chapter 7 – Corporate Culture and Exceptional Leadership. Employees of IDTC saw the everyday effect DCS policy initiatives were having on operations. Policy initiatives meant philosophy changes, rate cuts meant staffing adjustments, and the declining census jeopardized jobs. The stress of these changes took a toll on everyone. As the situation became more serious, some employees started looking for other jobs and some lost interest, and the degree of uncertainty undoubtedly affected the quality of the program and the atmosphere in the building.

On the other hand, the bad conditions brought out the best in some employees who rose to the occasion. To the last day, staff fought through the challenges of the job, knowing the ultimate outcome of their fate at exactly the same time many of the clients faced yet another uncertainty, thereby increasing their anxiety and potentially leading to more behavioral incidents. In the end, IDTC was able to navigate this situation without serious incident. The staff "pulled the rope in the same direction" under very difficult circumstances and acted responsibly to bring a dignified end to a noble program.

Discussion question: In what ways should you take different approaches to typical employee issues (e.g., missing a shift, being late, not completing documentation) leading to disciplinary action when a program is closing versus one that is operating normally?

Discussion question: What employee qualities become most important during a program closure?

_____

_____

_____

_____

_____

_____

Chapter 11 – Closing a Program. Closing a program is one of the most unpleasant tasks facing a human services professional. This usually occurs precisely when employees have the "least reserves in their tanks." A closure usually means the loss of jobs, security, and the ability to make a difference. The process can be highly emotional for all involved, and years of effort—designing systems, developing staff, and solving problems—disappear forever.

The decision to close the IDTC program was taken primarily for two reasons:

1. The Financial Reason. IDTC generated revenue from customers that referred children (the census). They paid a daily rate sufficient to cover direct costs and indirect costs, and to provide reinvestment capital (profit). Revenue was simply a multiplication equation: the daily rate times the census equaled total revenue. DCS was undermining both parts of the equation. IDTC once could control and calculate its daily rate under a free market approach, whereby a customer could choose to use IDTC or not. If a customer purchased services, IDTC would bring in the daily rate times the days purchased, and that would be the revenue. If a customer did not choose to conduct business with IDTC, then they would earn no revenue. This approach was simple and effective.

DCS fundamentally altered that dynamic by cutting rates of providers without discrimination. Sometimes DCS cut rates equally across a group of providers (for example, a 4% across-the-board rate cut). Sometimes these rate cuts purported to follow some kind of logic and varied by provider.

In the end, the rate cuts and rate uncertainty, combined with the declining census, proved to be the one-two punch that would have taken IDTC into the world of the "negative margin" and ultimately business failure.

2. The Philosophical Reason. The identified cause of the DCS rate cuts was the deterioration of the state of Indiana's economic picture and revenue projections. This was only partly true. The director of DCS was a very controlling individual with strong ideological views. IDTC managers believed the director would be in a position of authority for many years to come, perhaps even under the next governor (the existing governor was limited to two terms in office, ending in January 2013). The director believed in centralizing virtually every aspect of the entire out-of-home care system: authority over rate setting, admission to the DCS system, the emergency call system, placement authority, the provider network, policy changes, and the licensing process. He thereby sought to minimize the influence of local officials, such as juvenile judges and local

DCS offices who were most familiar with individual children and their needs. DCS also wanted to reward only those organizations that reflected its current philosophy.

DCS was distorting the reality of the situations of many of these children to fit the agency's view of the world. The general idea was that "all children should live with their (natural) families (including extended families)." DCS felt it should focus on providing family supports, and out-of-home care should be used rarely and only in extreme cases. This sounds sensible enough, but the issue for providers like IDTC was where the agency had decided to draw the line. The DCS goal to limit funding to a maximum of 500 out-of-home child placements statewide at any one time was, in the view of IDTC managers, a financial goal cloaked as a policy goal. This number was not based on need or reality but on budget. DCS used the financial crisis of 2008 to "adjust" DCS philosophy and to "adjust" the DCS state budget.

The financial reality for IDTC was that as rates and the DCS census numbers were dropping, revenue could only continue to drop. The trend line was particularly alarming, and it followed DCS official position changes very closely. It got to the point where IDTC considered whether it was appropriate and fair to its sister company programs to stay open, because it would be knowingly subsidizing a flawed funding system.

IDTC attempted to minimize the effects of the closure on the clients, families, guardians, employees, and other stakeholders to the extent it could. Their focus in the closure was to discharge 75 children within about 90 days with minimal effects to the IDTC reputation, the customer, their employees, and the children. Since Lafayette was staying open, it could continue to offer placement options to certain non-DCS customers. It was an additional goal for Lafayette to reduce DCS client count to a minimum (preferably zero by the beginning of 2013) and to retain children and relationships from non-DCS sources.

There was some confusion in the marketplace over the closure. Why does a great program choose to close? Was Lafayette closing also? What would happen to the children in their care? Was something else going on at IDTC that caused the closure? IDTC professional staff fielded these questions and many more. Of particular concern was the reaction of DCS officials to hearing about the closure. Would they retaliate via licensing, by removing Lafayette placements, or in other ways? IDTC relied on its behind-the-scenes lobbyists to scan the bureaucratic landscape for signs of trouble and to make preemptive strikes if any retaliation was observed.

We also had to contend with IDTC's financial and other stakeholders. The news of the closure was a shock to IDTC's bankers. At one time in the not-so-distant past, IDTC had generated healthy returns for the bottom line of the parent company. The bankers wondered if the industry was going to survive, how the company would weather the storm, and how the financials might deteriorate.

Closure of IDTC took place without any major problems, however, IDTC managers do not know the effects on the children who were discharged. After serving 800 children over the life of the program, IDTC perceived that the closure was more important to its staff than it was to its customers, DCS, the provider community, and the provider association. As in the movie *The Titanic*, the event was gut wrenching but once the ship was under water, the scene was very quiet—almost surreal. This caused some introspection. Was our vocation less important than we thought?

Discussion question: What are three reasons IDTC should have "waited out" the DCS situation and stayed open?

Discussion question: Did IDTC overreact in closing the program?

Discussion question: Why did IDTC close so quietly with no backlash, few condolences, and no apparent ramifications to the market or DCS?

Chapter 14 – Financial Management. Leading up to the DCS disaster, IDTC had internal discussions about the increasingly combative nature of its relationship with its largest customer. On one hand, DCS referrals remained strong, the relationship with licensing was positive, the case managers in the local DCS offices were supportive, and the rate was sufficient for the moment. The alarming rhetoric came from the central office. The question was who would win the battle of wills among the juvenile court judges, the local DCS offices, the children who needed care, and the DCS central office? About 90% of IDTC's annual revenue flowed from the state of Indiana, and

60% of its revenue came from DCS. DCS licensed 100% of IDTC beds. IDTC worried that DCS rate setting rules would eventually cover 100% of the Indiana revenue (90% of its total revenue) by also regulating the rates paid by the Indiana State Board of Education. Historically, the ISBOE paid free market rates that were close to the rates DCS was being charged before the implementation of rate regulation; however, ISBOE rates were driven by IDEA—education law DCS probably did not have to follow. Given all of this, revenue risks were great and the situation fluid.

If a small group of customers accounts for 100% of a provider's revenue, it assumes the business risk of its customer IN ADDITION TO the customer's own business risk, effectively doubling the risk (see page 149 of the text). In the case of IDTC, DCS decided to cut rates and slash placements for out-of-home care. DCS also began placing unreasonable demands upon IDTC in areas from recordkeeping to new, excessive reporting and licensing requirements. Another wrinkle was that DCS licensed the programs that enabled IDTC to serve non-DCS customers, and licensing issues in an extreme case could shut the program down.

After the closure, fortunately, IDTC was diversified enough to support the Lafayette location. To the extent possible, all customers were shifted to that location, and DCS census dropped to only 30 children (from a maximum of about 120 children in 2005). The plan for the future was to eliminate all DCS-funded children from programs by January 2013, absent a change in philosophy and direction by the agency. The ISBOE also continued to pay a separate, higher rate than DCS.

Discussion question: What would you have done to reduce the risk to IDTC from overexposure to DCS as a customer?

Discussion question: What would you have done if DCS daily rates were unacceptable, resulting in you having no DCS children in your care, and DCS refused to license your program, which was serving non-DCS clients?

Chapter 15 – Budgeting. The financial statement for IDTC for the six months ending June 30, 2012 (see Exhibit #2) shows that the budgeted contribution margin for the period starting January 1, 2012, and ending June 30, 2012 (the period containing the closure), was expected to be <$239,537>. The actual operating loss for the same period was actually <$377,980> for a contribution margin variance of <$138,443>.

Discussion question: What was the year-to-date (YTD) variance for "Total Income" between budget and actual at June 30, 2012?

_____

_____

_____

_____

_____

Discussion question: What was the YTD variance for "Total Direct Costs" between budget and actual at June 30, 2012?

_____

_____

_____

_____

_____

Discussion question: What was the YTD variance for "Total Indirect Costs" between budget and actual at June 30, 2012?

_____

_____

_____

_____

_____

Discussion question: What are the three financial accounts that can have the largest variances (either positive or negative)? Why do you think each of them occurred?

_____

_____

_____

_____

_____

_____

Chapter 18 – Rate Regulation. When DCS was spun off into a separate entity in 2005, the rate setting model was the free market. Providers were free to set the rates they needed for their operations. While no rate model is perfect, this one at least gave the provider the flexibility to adapt to the marketplace. The free market premise was simple: if you don't like the rate, don't use the services, and find another provider that offers you the services you want for a rate you will pay. This model was no different from any unregulated business (e.g., coffee, clothing, tools, accounting services, or legal services). Sometimes a provider would discount rates for a volume purchaser. But when money gets tight, rate regulation starts to sound more attractive and can be a focus of attention for a legislator or a bureaucrat seeking scarce budget dollars. Some regulators appear to believe those pesky providers are raking in money. Of course, for providers seeking to provide critical services while paying its direct care staff a livable wage, the reality is quite different.

Sometimes agencies use rate setting to achieve various public policy objectives that are not explicit. Telling the truth could be offensive to the public (i.e., the voter). In the case of IDTC, DCS instituted rate setting to achieve some specific objectives:

1. To weed out poor quality providers (decreasing the supply of beds AND eliminating "bad operators," as defined by DCS).
2. To decrease the supply of provider beds (efficiency).
3. To squeeze the vacancy out of the provider network (austerity).
4. To lower the profits or surpluses for the remaining provider network (austerity).
5. To decrease the size of the DCS budget on a permanent basis, allowing unspent funds to be returned to the general fund (this action gets the "gold star " for efficiency in government services),
6. To seek national publicity for outcomes (ideological).
7. To compel greater levels of in-home, family preservation, and kinship care services (ideological).

It was clear to IDTC that DCS rate regulation would constrain profitable market pricing. It was also clear that rate regulation would make it more difficult to satisfy customer expectations. IDTC had to avoid becoming a DCS-only program, eliminating services like behavioral health that ISBOE and out-of-state customers considered essential. IDTC also feared getting caught in a "death spiral" situation where the rate set by DCS does not allow the provider to generate a sufficient contribution margin or profit level. In the death spiral, the provider cuts costs to make ends meet and is "awarded" a rate that is even lower the following year for all its effort (see the death spiral example on page 209 of the text).

IDTC attempted to implement rate setting strategies that would offer the highest probability of rate success. The strategy was to: (1) try to reduce disallowances, (2) lower the divisor, (3) push back through its trade association, (4) use the court system, and (5) apply good business boundaries. These efforts were not enough for the Indianapolis campus of IDTC to remain open. It turned out that although the DCS 2013 rates were not perfect, they were sufficient to allow IDTC Lafayette to continue to serve a smaller group of DCS children.

Discussion question: What are two pros and two cons of rate regulation from the provider prospective?

Discussion question: What are two pros and two cons of rate regulation from the government prospective?

Discussion question: Give examples of how rate setting could constrain profitable market pricing.

Discussion question: Can you give examples of the disconnect among licensing, rate setting authorities, and the customer in a rate setting environment (see page 204 in the text)?

_____

_____

_____

_____

_____

_____

Discussion question: What strategy would you have used for IDTC to secure higher rates from DCS and why?

_____

_____

_____

_____

_____

_____

IDTC EXHIBIT #1

December 6, 1993

PROGRAM PURPOSE

There is an acute need for children's residential services in Marion County and the State of Indiana. There is an existing Marion County building, soon to be vacated, that is suitable for this use. Upon request of the Marion County officials, Oconomowoc Residential Programs, Inc. proposes to establish and operate a residential treatment program for children in the Marion County Health Care Center. This facility and our in depth special programming expertise, will allow Marion County to provide quality residential treatment care at a fiscally responsible cost.

FINANCIAL EFFECTS

There is a crisis in the State of Indiana related to child welfare and service delivery to children in need of treatment. Many articles have appeared in local newspapers over the last several years describing the child welfare problem. According to a Marion County legal opinion issued July 23, 1993, the state has identified about 7,000 children in need of residential treatment. Only a portion of these children are currently receiving services. Additional funding will not increase the availability of care in Indiana. According to IARCCA officials, their 2,800 beds in the state maintain full capacity. Approximately 500 Indiana children are placed in out-of-state facilities, at a cost of care that sometimes exceeds $300 per day per child. From January through May of 1992, approximately 34 children per month were sent to residential treatment centers out of state. This is an increase of 100% since 1990. Child welfare costs in Indiana counties have risen from $45 million in 1986 to $83 million in 1991. These figures do not include costs incurred by separate juvenile court budgets or costs of placements for education purposes.

In Marion County alone, approximately $30 million per year is being spent for residential treatment for children in need. This figure has doubled in the last several years. From a budget of approximately $66 million, $40.2 million is devoted to child welfare services versus a 1993 budget allotment of $29 million. That is a shortfall of over $10 million. Marion County Division of Family and Children projects a $19 million budget shortfall in 1993. It was $10 million over budget in 1992. Yet 700 children are identified as still needing residential treatment. See Appendix A.

The numbers of children in need of child welfare services and residential treatment services in particular is growing. Lack of resources, mandatory reporting of abuse and neglect, societal conditions, and other factors are contributing to an increasing need for the development of treatment alternatives for children. It is predicted that the numbers will continue to increase.

The conversion of the Marion County Health Care Center into a Residential Treatment Program for children operated by Oconomowoc Residential Programs, Inc. will provide:

1. A drastic reduction in taxpayer money leaving the county and the state for residential treatment services.

2. 250 new jobs within Marion County with a total annual payroll of $5.3 million.

3. An efficient use of a Marion county owned building that is projected to be vacant in January, 1995.

4. An option for earlier intervention, saving the county money over an identified resident's lifetime. (The philosophy is that early intervention may prevent future long-term needs for residential treatment; therefore, briefer treatment early on is more cost effective long-term.)

5. Lower per diem rates than many programs currently utilized by Marion County Division of Family and Children.

SERVICE DELIVERY EFFECTS

The establishment of this new local program enhances the entire delivery system of children's services in Marion County. The following benefits could be achieved:

1. This program would expand the number of Indiana beds providing residential treatment services for children. These beds are in short supply.

2. This program would provide total residential treatment to an identified population of dually-diagnosed children and young adults who are difficult to serve and not well suited for treatment in traditional facilities.

3. Children would be treated closer to home to enhance family involvement, family participation, and parental accountability.

4. This program would help to correct Indiana's failure to provide adequate or appropriate care for disturbed children locally.

5. This program would provide in-state services for children who require 24 hour care and treatment.

6. A local resource for serving a specific population of children with multiple problems and multiple handicapping conditions would be available. Children who are dually-diagnosed, developmentally disabled, have low incidence syndromes, neurologically handicapping conditions, and borderline MR conduct disorders would be served.

7. This facility could include a private secure unit for crisis management.

Exhibit 1

ORP

IDTC EXHIBIT #2

IDTC, LLC
BUDGET VS ACTUAL
For the Six Months Ending June 30, 2012
Summary of All Units

Account Description	Current Period			Year-To-Date			Annual
	Actual	Budget	Variance	Actual	Budget	Variance	Budget
Income							
Out of State Income	0	0	0	812,289	0	812,289	0
Respite Care Income	0	0	0	458	0	458	0
In State Income	0	0	0	2,235,227	2,687,557	(452,330)	2,687,557
Day School Income - In State	0	0	0	108,446	99,535	8,911	99,535
Management Fees Revenue	7,738	0	7,738	194,021	181,355	12,666	181,355
Rental Income	0	0	0	0	540	(540)	540
Total Income	**7,738**	**0**	**7,738**	**3,350,441**	**2,968,987**	**381,454**	**2,968,987**
Direct Care Staff Costs							
Salaries - Meals	161	0	(161)	55,309	38,897	(16,412)	38,897
Salaries - Clothing & Personal	3,330	0	(3,330)	70,681	67,550	(3,131)	67,550
Salaries - Direct Care	1,375	0	(1,375)	1,136,672	716,244	(420,428)	716,244
Salaries - Medical	165	0	(165)	74,038	51,435	(22,603)	51,435
Salaries - Social Services	0	0	0	58,909	70,402	11,493	70,402
Salaries - Education	113	0	(113)	139,553	124,380	(15,173)	124,380
Direct Care - Accrued PTO	(129)	0	129	(88,469)	0	88,469	0
Direct Care - Group Insurance	0	0	0	106,816	105,968	(848)	105,968
Direct Care - Workers Comp	3,886	0	(3,886)	78,310	44,014	(34,296)	44,014
Direct Care - Taxes + Oth Benefits	5,784	0	(5,784)	170,263	112,488	(57,775)	112,488
Recruitment Expenses	0	0	0	3,623	7,353	3,730	7,353
Staff Training	0	0	0	4,318	3,201	(1,117)	3,201
Total DC Staff Costs	**14,685**	**0**	**(14,685)**	**1,810,023**	**1,341,932**	**(468,091)**	**1,341,932**
% of Income	189.8%	0.0%	-189.8%	54.0%	45.2%	-8.8%	45.2%
Client Care Costs							
Meals and Entertainment - Direct	244	0	(244)	5,597	3,505	(2,092)	3,505
Food	22	0	(22)	66,898	61,000	(5,898)	61,000
Household Supplies	0	0	0	19,111	14,651	(4,460)	14,651
Personal Needs	0	0	0	1,645	3,430	1,785	3,430
Clothing	0	0	0	8,221	8,000	(221)	8,000
Allowances	0	0	0	1,960	2,742	782	2,742
Purchased Svc - Psychiatry	0	0	0	9,810	10,286	476	10,286
Purchased Svc - Clients	0	0	0	0	1,143	1,143	1,143
Purchased Svc - Assessments	0	0	0	0	3,430	3,430	3,430
Purchased Svc - Medical	2,000	0	(2,000)	13,881	8,000	(5,881)	8,000
Purchased Svc - Therapy	0	0	0	19,591	18,381	(1,210)	18,381
Purchased Svc - Dietary	0	0	0	791	1,143	352	1,143
Licenses and Fees	0	0	0	2,539	829	(1,710)	829
Linen and Household Furnishing	5,747	0	(5,747)	20,089	17,142	(2,947)	17,142
Medical Supplies	742	0	(742)	3,770	4,573	803	4,573
Recreation/Social Activities	65	0	(65)	7,224	8,572	1,348	8,572
Reinforcers	0	0	0	4,451	3,430	(1,021)	3,430

Exhibit 2, Page 1

Social Services Expenses	0	0	0	750	1,716	966	1,716
Therapy Expenses	0	0	0	744	231	(513)	231
Education Expenses	0	0	0	3,131	3,086	(45)	3,086
Total Client Care Costs	**8,820**	**0**	**(8,820)**	**190,203**	**175,290**	**(14,913)**	**175,290**
% of Income	114.0%	0.0%	-114.0%	5.7%	5.9%	0.2%	5.9%
Building & Grounds							
Salaries - Maintenance	689	0	(689)	81,518	64,996	(16,522)	64,996
Bldg Staff - Accrued PTO	(17)	0	17	(4,698)	0	4,698	0
Bldg Staff - Group Insurance	0	0	0	5,672	6,443	771	6,443
Bldg Staff - Workers Comp	521	0	(521)	4,158	2,676	(1,482)	2,676
Bldg Staff - Taxes + Oth Benefits	775	0	(775)	9,041	6,840	(2,201)	6,840
Building Rent-Related Party	7,260	7,260	0	528,935	528,935	0	572,495
Building Rent	0	0	0	2,032	1,675	(357)	1,675
Building Rent - Intercompany	3,657	3,417	(240)	20,741	20,502	(239)	23,919
Depr-Bldg, Leasehld, Furn/Fix	602	550	(52)	60,641	60,925	284	63,440
Building Mortgage Interest	0	0	0	7,290	6,604	(686)	6,604
Property Taxes	2,413	2,414	1	88,230	88,234	4	98,068
Insurance - Property	134	134	0	13,161	13,164	3	13,708
Repair & Maint - Bldg & Grounds	0	30,328	30,328	95,090	83,067	(12,023)	85,075
Purchased Svc - Bldg & Grounds	2,164	1,389	(775)	32,912	40,214	7,302	45,443
Building Utilities	(3,901)	1,640	5,541	86,861	92,172	5,311	98,042
Communications Expense	1,139	0	(1,139)	28,783	22,430	(6,353)	22,430
Equip Repairs & Maint	0	0	0	3,485	6,436	2,951	6,436
Equipment Rental	0	0	0	15,397	7,130	(8,267)	7,130
Equipment Lease Buyouts	0	0	0	4,208	0	(4,208)	0
Total Building Costs	**15,436**	**47,132**	**31,696**	**1,083,457**	**1,052,443**	**(31,014)**	**1,125,420**
% of Income	199.5%	0.0%	-199.5%	32.3%	35.4%	3.1%	37.9%
Transportation Costs							
Mileage - Direct	557	0	(557)	4,735	5,914	1,179	5,914
Client Travel	0	0	0	0	799	799	799
Auto Gas & Parking	361	0	(361)	16,969	10,286	(6,683)	10,286
Auto Repairs & Maint	0	0	0	6,862	6,314	(548)	6,314
Auto Leases	0	0	0	20,682	16,940	(3,742)	16,940
Insurance - Auto	0	0	0	6,525	6,525	0	6,525
Total Transportation	**918**	**0**	**(918)**	**55,773**	**46,778**	**(8,995)**	**46,778**
% of Income	11.9%	0.0%	-11.9%	1.7%	1.6%	-0.1%	1.6%
Total Direct Costs	**39,859**	**47,132**	**7,273**	**3,139,456**	**2,616,443**	**(523,013)**	**2,689,420**
% of Income	515.1%	0.0%	-515.1%	93.7%	88.1%	-5.6%	90.6%
Gross Profit $$	**(32,121)**	**(47,132)**	**15,011**	**210,985**	**352,544**	**(141,559)**	**279,567**
Gross Margin %	**-415.1%**	**0.0%**	**-415.1%**	**6.3%**	**11.9%**	**-5.6%**	**9.4%**
Indirect Costs							
Salaries - Mgmt & General	10,308	0	(10,308)	417,698	408,745	(8,953)	408,745
Deferred Comp Expense	1,154	0	(1,154)	12,742	8,722	(4,020)	8,722
Indirect Staff - Accrued PTO	(288)	0	288	(24,806)	0	24,806	0
Indirect Staff - Group Insurance	0	0	0	29,950	41,386	11,436	41,386
Indirect Staff - Workers Comp	8,660	0	(8,660)	21,957	17,190	(4,767)	17,190
Indirect Staff - Taxes + Oth Benefits	12,888	0	(12,888)	47,740	43,933	(3,807)	43,933
Bad Debts	0	0	0	5,714	0	(5,714)	0

Exhibit 2, Page 2

Publicity & Marketing	0	0	0	645	0	(645)	0
Employee Recognition	3	0	(3)	1,848	3,114	1,266	3,114
GAP Match	91	0	(91)	1,196	103	(1,093)	103
Dues/Memberships/Subscriptions	0	0	0	6,401	3,759	(2,642)	3,759
Insurance - General/Liability	1,825	1,825	0	32,490	32,490	0	39,400
Postage	0	0	0	2,728	2,857	129	2,857
Other Interest	0	0	0	0	15	15	15
Depreciation - Office Equip	19	19	0	1,986	2,104	118	2,123
Purchased Svc - Audit Fees	0	0	0	11,529	6,001	(5,528)	6,001
Purchased Svc - Legal	4,465	0	(4,465)	(1,003)	5,657	6,660	5,657
Office Supplies & Expenses	2,982	0	(2,982)	11,058	5,840	(5,218)	5,840
Computers and Supplies	0	0	0	1,367	5,405	4,038	5,405
Computer Licenses	0	0	0	600	0	(600)	0
Travel and Lodging	3,190	0	(3,190)	6,978	4,760	(2,218)	4,760
Miscellaneous Non Allowable	0	0	0	147	0	(147)	0
Total Indirect Costs	**45,297**	**1,844**	**(43,453)**	**588,965**	**592,081**	**3,116**	**599,010**
% of Income	585.4%	0.0%	-585.4%	17.6%	19.9%	2.4%	20.2%
Program Margin $$	**(77,418)**	**(48,976)**	**(28,442)**	**(377,980)**	**(239,537)**	**(138,443)**	**(319,443)**
Program Margin %	**-1000.5%**	**0.0%**	**-1000.5%**	**-11.3%**	**-8.1%**	**-3.2%**	**-10.8%**
Contribution Margin	**(77,418)**	**(48,976)**	**(28,442)**	**(377,980)**	**(239,537)**	**(138,443)**	**(319,443)**
CM %	**-1000.49%**	**0.00%**	**-1000.49%**	**-11.28%**	**-8.07%**	**-3.21%**	**-10.76%**

Exhibit 2, Page 3

NOTES

NOTES

LICENSING AND RULE-MAKING AUTHORITY

Background

Jeff is a middle manager working for a human services company that runs community-based programs for adults with various disabilities and impairments. He has four direct reports who directly supervise an assortment of living arrangements, from group homes to apartment programs, serving about 55 individuals in total. One of the group homes he is responsible for serves clients who are afflicted with significant eating disorders whose condition, without proper management and supports, would likely lead to death. Another serves a group of individuals with developmental disabilities. About half of these individuals have significant behavioral problems that coexist with their developmental disability. Jeff reports to a regional supervisor who oversees the care for almost 250 individuals.

The quarterly financial review is drawing near. Jeff's two programs are not margining well, even though the lives of the individuals being served have been significantly enhanced compared to previous placements. Jeff has added extra staff to monitor the kitchen in one of the homes and to manage the behaviors and provide backup in the other. He knows what is going to happen when he and his supervisor meet to discuss the financials, and he worries that good programs might close for reasons that could be prevented. He is also concerned about where the clients would go. He wants to resolve this situation once and for all.

Situation #1

Licensing has a certain "DNA" that focuses on licensee responsibilities, treatment and care, resident rights, the physical environment, and safety. Licensing requirements can be onerous at times and can actually interfere with a successful community placement. A licensing rule that might seem reasonable could have very negative consequences for certain individuals in the one-size-fits-all world of licensing. Jeff was thinking about the truth of this statement and decided he had to do something about it. He knew he could blame licensing for his problem, he could blame his supervisor for not solving his problem, or he could take responsibility for finding a solution.

What exactly was Jeff's problem? Jeff was serving individuals with a genetic eating disorder, a disorder so insidious that it would ultimately lead to death from overeating if left untreated. Among the treatment protocols was strict food regulation, which provided external controls to supplant the internal biological controls these people lacked.

This required either:

1. Locking food supplies in the house (which plainly violated the resident rights protections in the licensing code).

2. Staffing the kitchen during all the hours the clients were in the house (a budget buster that would have effectively ended the community placement and forced the clients to return to a more restrictive setting).

3. Dealing with the negative results unencumbered food access would present on a one-by-one basis (threatening the clients' safety and exposing the company to increased risk).

Jeff had heard of "reasonable accommodation" in the organization as it related to a zoning case the company undertook in years past and wondered if it might be a useful tool in this case. Jeff also knew that there were some simple ways to minimize the probability of a bad outcome and enhance the likelihood of a good one. He decided to approach licensing and ask for an exception to the rule that prohibited food restriction. He also asked for an exception to the rule that prohibited the locking of food supplies within the home. He knew:

1. He would have to describe the problem in a way that both licensing and the agency could agree was true.
2. He would have to provide the facts based on numbers because numbers tend not to shade the truth.
3. He would have to "own" his opinions, which were interpretations of the facts.
4. He would have to recommend actions that were very specific.
5. He had to ensure that licensing comprehended the problem and the recommended solution.
6. He would have to be ready for challenges and pushback from the bureaucrats.

Jeff understood that when all was said and done, the goal was not to diminish Licensing or the job they do, but to end the conversation with integrity and compassion (yes, compassion) for their position, with the goal of walking away with a workable solution to the problem.

Discussion question: What should Jeff do if Licensing denies his variance request to lock up food?

Discussion question: Give three examples of how this regulatory oversight and open access to food could affect rates.

_____

_____

_____

_____

_____

_____

Discussion question: Give three examples of increased risk to the company if the request is denied.

_____

_____

_____

_____

_____

_____

Discussion question: What would have been the likely outcome had Jeff blamed his supervisor for not solving the problem or blamed Licensing, rather than taking responsibility for solving the problem?

_____

_____

_____

_____

_____

_____

Situation #2

Jeff faces a problem in another group home. The program is in a side-by-side duplex with developmentally disabled (DD) behavioral clients on one side and the non-behavioral DD clients living in the other. The license is issued for the whole property as if it were one large house, even though some internal segregation by client type occurs. This arrangement enhances the treatment and care for these individuals and offers improved safety and less disruption for the clients if one client has a bad day.

Licensing has been rumbling about the effects a few clients are having on resident rights requirements and the physical environment that has been adapted to accommodate the behavioral clients. Specifically, Licensing does not approve of closing the door that that was installed between the two living units, which is useful when events get active on the behavioral side of the program. Jeff has asked the customer for funds for coverage during the hours of peak activity, including for late night activity, because one client has significant problems with insomnia. His staffing request was denied. In fact, the customer notified Jeff recently that it has completed updated assessments on its clients and has decided that all four clients that reside in the home (of the eight clients total from three different customers) will be getting rate decreases of 15% each starting in two months. Jeff knows that this will make a bad situation worse. He wants to be prepared with a solution to the problem when he meets with his supervisor to review the financials in a few weeks.

Discussion question: Provide an example of how Licensing (a government agency) and the customer (the same agency but a different department) could work together to solve Jeff's problem.

Discussion question: At what point would the company be forced to discharge some of the behavioral residents?

Discussion question: List three things preventing Licensing and the customer from working with Jeff to help solve the problem in a way that is in the best interest of the clients.

Discussion question: How can Jeff strategically position both Licensing and the customer (the same government agency) to solve their problem without Jeff getting in the middle?

NOTES

NOTES

PROFIT FROM THE CORE

Background

For almost 40 years, Genesee Lake School (GLS, formerly ODTC) has served children with developmental disabilities and emotional disturbances in a residential setting, with customers from a handful of states. It has amassed a significant amount of intellectual property and market goodwill for serving what had become known by the children's court judges as "the Oconomowoc type of kid."

Over the past 20 years, the more traditional models of residential treatment that emerged in the 1960s, 1970s, and 1980s have evolved into less restrictive community-based alternatives and family options. By the mid-1990s, some leaders of ODTC thought that the organization was stuck in time and at risk of becoming obsolete due to its lack of emphasis on Individuals with Disabilities Education Act (IDEA) and the new wave of education laws and emerging markets. Others were of the view that ODTC, with a clear focus on human services funded by human services budgets, would continue to be a viable company only if it expanded its geographic reach to more states. Some advocated the later approach but suggested greater specialization and distinction in the marketplace as a way to grow and prosper. Finally, some thought that nothing needed to change.

The strategic issues became urgent as:

1. Placements were becoming shorter, dropping from an average length of stay of 24 months to 18 months or less over the last five years.

2. Human services budgets were projected to decrease or, at best, hold flat.

3. Policy makers preferred home and community-based options to out-of-home care.

4. States were looking to bring revenue back home from out-of-state placements. These forces pointed to continuing revenue and margin pressure for the company. Something needed to change; the question was what.

The Process

The company undertook a process whereby key staff attempted to slice and dice the ODTC business to develop a strategy for the future. The task was to:

1. Identify its core business in terms of profitable customers, strategic capabilities, critical service offerings, and market channels.

2. Focus on its core business, seeking to build it to its full potential.

3. Subject to available capital, develop new adjacent business in market spaces that had the best probability of success.

The Core Business. The team decided that the core business of ODTC consisted of residential treatment and education services that specialized in populations of children that had co-occurring developmental disabilities (DD) and emotional disturbances (ED). These children would not fit into traditional DD programs due to their ED behaviors and would not fit into traditional ED programs due to their DD and intellectual challenges.

The profitable customers increasingly tended to be focused on education, probably due to the strength of IDEA, which was gaining traction as a major driver of referral business. In addition, services for children from Wisconsin counties tended to be profitable due to a free market rate environment and a reluctance to use out-of-state vendors. Certificate of Need (CON) regulations made it impossible to develop new beds, further restricting supply.

ODTC had unique strategic capabilities and expertise in the area of behavior management and emotional regulation. Its services were sufficiently distinct that the market—case managers, local judges, and human services departments—actually blended the name with the child, referring to someone as "the Oconomowoc type of kid" on a regular basis.

Focusing on the Core. Once management agreed on the definition of the core business, the next question was how to build the core to its full potential. The team looked at expanding markets, ways to improve operations, and possible innovations in its core services. The analysis proceeded in steps:

1. The first step related to bed availability in the main complex. ODTC traditionally has had few vacancies. The State of Wisconsin had, and still has, a CON process that served as a gate through which all agencies had to pass before they could expand the bed supply. Limited beds represented a major hurdle to expanding markets and increasing revenue.

2. A second step was to explore providing more of the core services in another location. It was easy to see that this alternative would be so expensive that it could not be considered. Finding another location with a similar infrastructure would trigger such substantial start-up expenses that it could not be an option except for a company with very deep pockets.

Another factor made starting a program in another state undesirable. Wisconsin was (and is) a "uniform fee" state. If IDTC expanded into another state, they would lose the protections afforded to them from uniform fee code for their out-of-state customers. The uniform fee code states that "no purchaser may pay a lesser rate than the Wisconsin published daily rate." This meant that out-of-state customers had to "pay to play," with no exceptions.

3. A third step was to consider ways they could improve existing operations that would assure a strong future flow of business that the competition could not touch. After a thorough analysis, the team decided ODTC should focus on enhancement of their education program because IDEA could drive business their way. This required an investment in educational infrastructure at a cost approaching six million dollars. The team believed this would give them the best shot at weathering the long-term decline that was anticipated in national human services budgets. The team also thought it would provide a way to distinguish ODTC in the marketplace by adding yet another layer of expertise: education. Along with a renewed emphasis on the natural beauty of ODTC and the esthetically pleasing physical plant, the elements of the new strategic direction took shape.

Expanding into Adjacent Businesses. Building market power in a well-defined core is the key source of competitive advantage and represents the most viable and least risky approach to business expansion. But the ODTC team thought that a push beyond the boundaries of the core business could leverage future business opportunities. The team analyzed thoroughly all of the opportunities that were distinct from, but related, to the core. A visual depiction of the final product that the team produced is located on page 216 of the text. ODTC decided it had the capabilities to rely on its core competencies to expand into the services shown in the first concentric ring of the map:

1. Residential only
2. Day school (placing an emphasis on the enhanced education program)
3. Day vocational services
4. Specialty group homes
5. Training (intellectual property)
6. In-home community-based services
7. Educational consulting
8. Behavioral consulting
9. Early childhood programming
10. Diagnostic and evaluation services
11. Respite services

The management group clearly had enough opportunities from which to choose. How should they decide which opportunities to pursue? For each, they considered:

1. *How much start-up investment was needed?*
2. *What was the likelihood of adjacent business success?*
3. *How much internal expertise was present in the core?*
4. *Was there a project champion already?*
5. *Would the adjacency detract focus from the core and result in "core drift"?*
6. *What was the probability of the adjacent business driving referrals to the core?*
7. *What was the margin potential in the adjacent business?*
8. *Was the adjacent business a "loss leader" that nevertheless would provide value to the core that would more than offset the losses?*

Discussion question: Of the adjacent business opportunities listed, name three that you think would require the most start-up capital. Why?

_____

_____

_____

_____

_____

_____

_____

Discussion question: Which three adjacencies do you think would have the highest probability of success? Why?

_____

_____

_____

_____

_____

_____

_____

Discussion question: Which three adjacencies do you think would have the highest margin potential? Why?

_____

_____

_____

_____

_____

_____

_____

Discussion question: Which adjacency do you think is likely to be a "loss leader" (one that has a negative margin but that drives profitable business to the core)? Why?

NOTES

NOTES

PUBLIC POLICY AND THE LEGAL SYSTEM: THE 2,500-FOOT RULE

Background

Medicaid funds are the main source of support for individuals with developmental disabilities. These funds provide care for nearly half a million individuals in the United States. The passage of the ICF/MR law (Medicaid Title XIX, 1971) enabled states to secure federal matching funds for various types of programs, dramatically increasing the supply of available beds for individuals with disabilities.

Progress continued when Congress first authorized the Home and Community Based Services (HCBS) Waiver in 1981. This triggered a radical change in the service delivery system. The waiver contemplated a wide range of service delivery types for developmentally disabled (DD) populations that would be authorized by state-by-state "waiver plans"—plans that sought permission to waive strict Medicaid rules. Each state submitted such plans to the U.S. Center for Medicaid Services for review, potential suggestions for modifications, and approval. Wisconsin's plan, modified numerous times over the years, includes Medicaid Waiver funding for case management, assistive technologies, homemaker assistance, home health, personal cares, residential services, day programs, respite care, transportation, supported employment, home modifications, and various therapies.

For HIL, Medicaid Waiver was a game changer. With the decline of the mental health market due to the Omnibus Budget Reconciliation Act (OBRA) of 1981 during the Reagan administration, an austerity measure intended to reduce domestic spending; HIL was on the lookout for new business. OBRA effectively ended federal funding for community treatment for the mentally ill, and shifted the burden almost exclusively to the individual states. This meant HIL had few alternatives for new business outside of the new waiver world.

Bed Sell Homes and the 2,500-Foot Rule

By the early 1990s, HIL had developed a "bed sell" model for its community living arrangements, selling each bed to a customer instead of selling a complete group home or one-twelfth (1/12) contract to individual counties for assorted programs. This alternative business model meant that a purchaser did not have to commit to purchasing all the beds in a group home, thereby absorbing any vacancy that tended to drive up the daily rate per day of care. The county could purchase only the days of care that it needed, leaving the vacancy risk to HIL. HIL had a head start in the race to grow services and sales, as other providers were slow to catch on to the bed sell model. However, HIL was beginning to have difficulty locating community living arrangements (CLAs) in "open" areas, limiting its ability to grow rapidly.

By law, an open area was an area of a municipality in Wisconsin that was "not within 2,500 feet of another community living arrangement" as the crow flew. This was a problem for HIL. The

2,500-foot rule was in a state law passed in 1977. It was initially a good law with appropriate intentions behind it. It broke down the municipal barriers used to block individuals with afflictions such as mental health, developmental disabilities, aging, and physical disabilities from living in regular neighborhoods. It was intended to minimize the effects of bigotry, (i.e., "not in my backyard" or "no business in a residential area") excuses that were popular in preventing CLAs from locating in community-based settings. It also prevented the re-segregation of people with disabilities into clusters in community settings.

Restrictions on Growth

By the early 1990s, HIL and other Wisconsin providers encountered more and more difficulty finding an open area, i.e., an area that was more than 2,500 feet from another CLA. The law that was once noble had become a law that was bad for business and bad for the disabled. Waiver clients demanded beds, but HIL could not find suitable locations to open CLAs. Making the problem worse, state centers were downsizing, and more and more individuals with disabilities were moving into CLAs. Compounding the problem was that the rule also applied to programs for the elderly.

HIL faced a dilemma. Should it take proactive steps to challenge the state law, or should it wait for a trade association or another provider to do so? If HIL decided to take some action, should that be legislative, executive, or judicial?

After almost 20 years of CLA growth, open areas were becoming increasingly scarce, and most proposed programs were within 2,500 of another CLA, many times an elderly program. Agencies proposing CLAs within 2,500 feet of one another had to seek a municipal variance in an onerous process. Such waivers were rarely granted without a battle. The weapon of choice in those battles was the Americans with Disabilities Act, or ADA (1990). The ADA bars discrimination against people with disabilities in employment, public service, and public accommodations. The ADA confirmed, once and for all, that discrimination against people with disabilities in the form of purposeful unequal treatment within historical patterns of segregation and isolation was the major problem confronting people with disabilities rather than the individual impairments.

One by one, HIL located an appropriate property to house a CLA and tussled with municipal officials and neighborhood groups using the threat of ADA and its "reasonable accommodations" clause. This process was slow, expensive, and labor intensive. The lead times in opening a CLA were a year or more. HIL typically won these battles in the end, and it feared the fallout that backing down might have had on its reputation in other communities.

The Last Straw

In 1996, the Wisconsin biennial state budget featured state match money to fund Medicaid Waiver slots for more than one hundred individuals with traumatic brain injuries (TBIs). HIL was also hopeful that the next biennial budget would include more TBI line-item funding. State match line-item funding does not roll forward into the next budget cycle; it must be budgeted again if not spent. HIL also knew that once TBI placements occurred, there would be a high likelihood that sufficient waiver funding would follow for the rest of the lives of those individuals.

The race was on. As the clock ticked, HIL could no longer suffer a lead time of one year or more to open a CLA as municipal officials challenged every step of the process. HIL did not have enough staff to accelerate the zoning battles that were becoming par for the course. HIL had to take a stand and eliminate the municipality battles from the start-up equation to open enough CLAs before the TBI waiver funds dried up. HIL was alarmed that it would miss the opportunity for 25, 50, or even 75 lifetime TBI CLA placements.

The City of Greenfield Lawsuit

HIL desired to open a group home (CLA) in a residential area following the criteria discussed in Chapter 23 (Real Estate) in the text. A suitable location was found in Greenfield, Wisconsin. It was a one-level home suitable for conversion to wheelchair accessibility and would be used to house individuals with acquired TBI funded by the new Medicaid Waiver. This raised two issues: (1) HIL would need to get a building permit to make the accessibility changes necessary to serve the population (HIL had a history of delayed response or no response to building permit requests from municipalities), and (2) the city required that HIL could only open a program if it received a variance to operate a group home as dictated in the municipal zoning code.

HIL was denied the variance and sued the city for violating its rights under the Fair Housing Amendments Act of 1988, the Americans with Disabilities Act of 1990, and the Equal Protection Clause of the Fourteenth Amendment (Case No. 96-C-1112 United States District Court, E.D. Wisconsin). This effort took over a year of staff time and cost upwards of $100,000 in legal fees. On September 30, 1998, HIL prevailed in a decision that: (1) did not invalidate the 2,500-foot rule, but (2) found that the statute limited meaningful access to housing for a disabled person (i.e., it was preempted by ADA and the Fair Housing Amendments Act), and (3) ordered the proposed zoning variance granted as a "reasonable accommodation" to the rights of the disabled residents. The pattern of harassment, discrimination, and delay by municipal officials was coming to an end. Now HIL and other providers had a legal decision they could invoke to persuade municipal officials to act in a timely fashion and make the right decision for individuals with disabilities. This case also paved the way for other providers to make headway in opening programs in settings that required municipal permits or zoning permissions.

The City of Milwaukee Lawsuit

The fight, however, was not yet over. When the City of Milwaukee denied a zoning variance to operate a group home for brain injured and developmentally disabled individuals, HIL returned to the legal arena. This time it sued the City of Milwaukee for violations of the Fair Housing Amendments Act and the ADA. On appeal (Case No. 01-1002 United States Court of Appeals, Seventh Circuit, decided August 8, 2002) the circuit judge held that: (1) the city's system of permitting group homes in single family districts did not provide a "reasonable accommodation" to disabled persons, and (2) the granting of a zoning variance was reasonable and necessary to provide individuals with an equal opportunity to enjoy housing in a residential area.

This battle ultimately consumed five years of staff time in legal preparations and close to $400,000 more in legal fees. In the meantime, prospective clients were backed up in nursing homes waiting for their opportunity for community placement and the Medicaid Waiver funding that would follow them for the rest of their lives. Fortunately, HIL was awarded damages and legal fees that approached $500,000.

The Conclusion

That is still not the complete story. Even before the City of Milwaukee case was affirmed on appeal, municipalities were beginning to understand that local zoning codes were no match for the federal laws that secured the rights of those with disabilities. By 1999, HIL and other organizations were making headway in opening other programs that would have been blocked before. Municipal interference was on the decline, but it took these two court cases to pave the way for organizations like HIL to provide the program opportunities that Medicaid Waiver afforded those with disabilities.

It is a sad footnote that these opportunities came too late for those who would have qualified for lifetime Medicaid TBI Waiver funding. By 1999, Wisconsin had eliminated the special TBI state match. Much of it was left unspent. Individuals who could have benefited from timely opening of these programs remained in nursing homes years longer than necessary, their lives forever altered by the "not in my backyard" mentality and discrimination that flourished throughout the state.

Discussion question: Do you think HIL should have filed the lawsuit? Please give three reasons for your answer.

_____

_____

_____

_____

_____

_____

Discussion question: What branch of government, other than the legal branch, could HIL have pursued to seek to eliminate the effects of the 2,500-foot rule? Explain what you would have done.

_____

_____

_____

_____

_____

_____

Discussion question: Do you think HIL should have looked for other business opportunities to replace the lost mental health business that would not have required fighting municipalities over the 2,500-foot rule? Name three other markets they could have targeted.

Discussion question: Knowing what you know now, was the lawsuit fight worth it for HIL? Why or why not?

NOTES

NOTES

THE RICHARDSON SCHOOL

Case Overview

The Richardson School (TRS) is a 65-student day school for special needs children located in West Allis, Wisconsin. It opened for business in March 2011. The purpose of the school is to provide an exceptional learning environment for a certain population of children who are marginalized in a public school setting.

Federal law (EHCA – 1975 / IDEA 1990) guarantees that children and youth with disabilities have the right to a "free appropriate public education." Those legislative actions afforded parents, for the first time, a federal right to secure an adequate public education for their children with disabilities. Parents and students could now seek enforcement of those rights in administrative proceedings and in the courts if they believed their rights were being violated.

When education laws were first passed in the 1970s, it did not necessarily follow that the funding was there to support those rights. In fact, it is not uncommon for the federal government to issue requirements to state or local governments, without providing any funding to back up the services. This phenomenon is known as an "unfunded mandate" and it is regularly used in the human service delivery system, as well as in other areas of federal/state regulation.

Federal education legislation called for the federal government eventually to fund special education in the ratio 40% federal/60% state. That means the federal government would need to give the states 40 cents for every dollar they spent to comply with the mandates. Yet the federal match funding is currently stuck at about 17 cents on the dollar—far short of the original intent of Congress. This match can only be altered by Congress and this is unlikely to occur in the current budget environment. These issues place extreme financial stress on local public school districts that are charged with educating ALL children who walk through their doors.

Therein lies the opportunity for TRS. If, through subcontract, TRS can educate these special needs children (1) in a way that helps a public school district follow the letter and spirit of the law by successfully educating all children, (2) in a more cost-effective way than the public school can perform this task itself, (3) with better academic outcomes than can be achieved in the public school setting, and (4) while satisfying parents and creating champions for TRS—we produce a win/win/win, for the child, the public school, and for TRS. That is the value proposition.

Analysis By Chapter

Chapter 1 – The History of Disability. Historically children with impairments were not educated; they were segregated, locked up, or worse. As a result of the social upheaval of the 1950s and 1960s, the Kennedy Commission on Mental Retardation, and the Civil Rights movement, individual rights for people with impairments were greatly strengthened. These what factors, along with the independent living initiatives and self-advocacy movements of the 1970s, culminated in legal protections that paved the way for TRS.

Discussion question: Do you think there was a market for the types of educational services provided by TRS in the United States in the early 20th century? If so, what social constructs prohibited the TRS educational offering?

Chapter 2 – Important Cases, Laws, and Watershed Events. The market for these education services exists, in the legal sense, because of at least three major pieces of federal legislation:

1. Section 504 of the Rehabilitation Act (1973), which prohibits entities receiving federal funding from discriminating against people with disabilities.

2. IDEA (1975), which guarantees children and youth the right to a free appropriate public education.

3. The ADA (1990), which bars discrimination against people with disabilities in employment, public service, and most importantly for public schools, in public accommodations. These laws quite literally drive the demand and therefore the market. Without a strong legal basis, students and parents would be at a distinct disadvantage when seeking education services. Note that these laws do not apply to private or religious schools.

Discussion question: What are three ways that TRS would be impacted if these acts didn't exist?

Discussion question: Do you think the lack of these laws could prove fatal to the TRS business model?

_____

_____

_____

_____

_____

_____

Chapter 3 – Public Policy. The funding for public schools has come under attack in recent years. Buyers of services from TRS generally come from only two places: (1) a public school or public school district, or (2) private pay families (sometimes, not always, awaiting the results of litigation). School voucher programs are expanding and gaining traction fueled by court cases and political support. This could increase financial stress on public schools by leaving behind the higher cost students with less money to educate them.

Discussion question: What are three ways you think the voucher program will help or hurt the market for TRS?

_____

_____

_____

_____

_____

_____

_____

_____

_____

Chapter 4 – Agency Mission. The OFC mission statement indicates a mission of "being the provider of choice for people with disabilities." Educating children and youth afflicted with intellectual disabilities fits perfectly within this mission. OFC has the expertise, the financial ability, and the desire to serve school-age children who seek an alternative educational opportunity in a non-traditional public school setting. Indeed, it is part of the company's DNA to pursue these types of services. So long as there is funding, the odds of success will be high.

Discussion question: Name three competitive advantages that are realized by following your mission statement when opening or expanding into a new business.

_____

_____

_____

_____

_____

_____

Chapter 6 – Organizational Structure. When opening a new program the proper organizational structure is critical to its success. TRS was created as a separate LLC corporation owned by the human services parent corporation and a separate profit center. It is also part of a controlled group because the stock of TRS is wholly owned by a parent company. Separate incorporation helps TRS to create its own identity, and commit 100% of its effort towards the new school. TRS could have been set up as a department of an affiliated residential treatment program Genesee Lake School (GLS) that also provides education services, but the concern was that if done, the focus would be diluted. The organizational structure of TRS tends toward being of "mechanistic" design (see page 44 of the text). Its vertical specialization and control, tight rules, greater standardization, and centralized staff assure operating objectives, quality standards, and customer satisfaction is achieved. This works well in an education environment with public school customers because they have very specific contract standards and performance expectations. Some aspects of the organizational structure resemble the "matrix" design (see page 43 of the text), with "dual reporting" to both the functional supervisor and the operations director who are on site. The departments of finance, marketing, human resources, and information systems services are operated in this manner.

Discussion question: Do you think TRS should be operated as a department of GLS or operated as a separate entity? Please state your preference and explain at least three factors that were most important to you when making your choice.

_____

_____

_____

_____

_____

_____

Chapter 7 – Corporate Culture and Exceptional Leadership. The operations director and business manager of the school were selected from the staff of a related company, GLS. Management understood that this start-up required a leader with a unique set of skills and leadership qualities, who could model the skills necessary to develop an exceptional leadership team. It was believed this individual did not absolutely need a background in education, but most importantly needed passion, confidence, and an ability to overcome unforeseen obstacles that are an inevitable part of the new business process. By incorporating separately, management also sent a message that the new leaders of TRS could develop their own culture, which would likely be different in some ways from the culture of GLS. By virtue of geographic differences alone, it was likely the cultures of the two companies would vary. GLS is forty-five miles outside of Milwaukee, in a rural/suburban environment, while TRS stands amid a densely populated urban area. With no residential program, the TRS team would also learn to navigate the unique requirements of a day school.

Discussion question: Compare and contrast two cultural and leadership issues that will arise if TRS and GLS function as a combined entity. Compare and contrast as a separate entity.

Chapter 9 – Opening a New Program. The idea for TRS was floating around the research and development efforts of the parent company for at least 10 years before action was taken to implement the idea. The R&D function was a "skunk works" for new program ideas that built on the services the company already was performing. The company, however, had no formal system to evaluate, develop, and open new services other than those that might occur through organic growth. For many years, this did not appear to be a problem, since there were so many organic growth opportunities that little planning was needed for the company to grow steadily and substantially. But when the recession and the financial crisis occurred, traditional growth opportunities ground to a halt, exposing gaps in the company's ability to find new opportunities. Only those programs that enjoyed a strong internal champion were opening. As pressure grew on operations to stretch their dollars, there was reluctance to take a chance on a new program with an unproven history. Ideas remained ideas.

As the idea for TRS was considered, the value proposition was discussed: Why would a customer purchase their services? The short answer was that TRS could educate children with certain types of special needs (1) for less money than public schools were spending, while (2) achieving better academic progress as shown by standardized testing, and (3) the children would demonstrate measurably better behavior. In mathematical terms, if the benefit to the school of using TRS, less the cost of the TRS daily rate, was positive, TRS provided value to the public school and it should elect to use TRS services (Benefits – Cost = Value).

Sometimes there is value that cannot easily be associated with a dollar number. In the case of TRS, this came through in value such as reduction of "administrative headaches," a reduction in complaints from teachers and parents of other children, and general relief that TRS has taken care of a school's significant problem area.

Discussion question: Value propositions usually revolve around the following: superior performance, customization, price, cost reduction, convenience, and outcomes. Which items are the most relevant in the value proposition of TRS and why?

_____

_____

_____

_____

_____

_____

_____

_____

_____

If the cost/benefit proposition for the school was positive, the question for TRS became whether its revenue would exceed the cost of providing the service (Revenue – Cost = Contribution Margin).

Critical to starting any new human services program is a sound financial analysis. TRS made its best and most educated guesses as to (1) how long it would take to get to a normalized state, (2) what was the operating margin once TRS reached normalization, (3) what were the maximum likely cumulative losses and maximum cash outflows during the start-up, and (4) how long would it take to recoup the start-up losses and begin to generate overall profitability from the project (see Exhibit #1).

Discussion question: In what period does TRS break even (refer to Exhibit #1)?

_____

_____

Discussion question: What is the cumulative start-up loss at the end of year 1 (refer to Exhibit #1)?

_____

_____

Discussion question: In what period does the cumulative profit offset the start-up losses (refer to Exhibit #1)?

_____

_____

Discussion activity: Complete the start-up graph using the TRS budget in Exhibit #1.

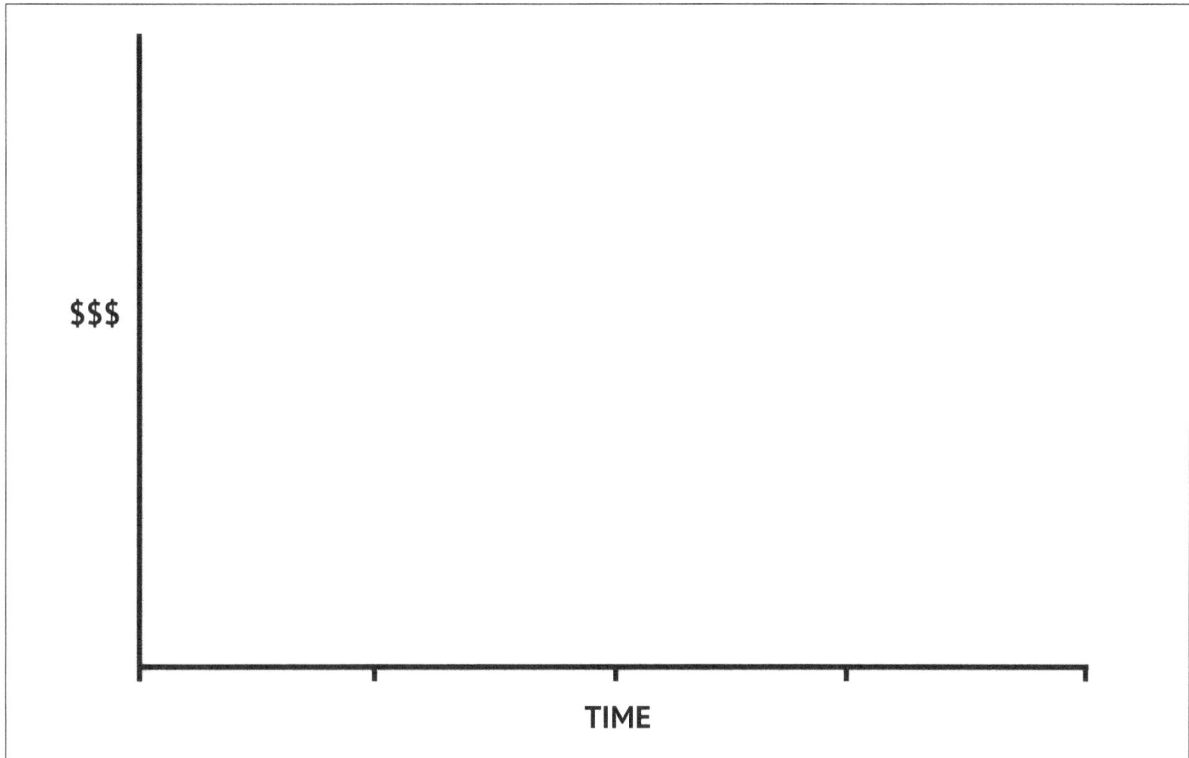

Start-Up Graph: Include Start-Up Loss, Fixed Costs, Variable Costs, Revenue, Breakeven Point, and Operating Profit

Discussion question: Using the graph, can you explain why "time is money" (refer to Exhibit #1 and see page 75 in the text)?

_____

_____

The location of TRS would be critical to its success. The team decided that the location should satisfy some very specific criteria:

1. It should be within an urban area that had many school districts that were prospective customers to support the dispersion of revenue.

2. It should be within an area with an established bus system that could transport children (one of the most expensive of education services).

3. It should be centrally located so customers could approach the site from all directions using normal transportation methods.

4. It should be within an area with a qualified workforce.

Discussion question: What do you think is the MOST important factor to consider in the locating of a school like TRS?

_____

_____

_____

_____

_____

_____

The TRS team also had to address the very real possibility that sometimes good programs just do not survive. Research shows that most business failures occur within the first three years of operation (usually in year 3). In the spirit of "no denial" and being accountable, the team took several steps to minimize the downside risk. First, long-term exposure to hard assets such as real estate and equipment was limited, through the use of more flexible leasing arrangements. Second, key employees who had been recruited from other family companies were assured that if the venture did not succeed, they could re-integrate with positions in the other companies, thereby limiting their career risk. Third, a separate name was assigned to TRS to avoid any reputational fall-out for GLS if the venture did not work.

Discussion question: What are at least three reasons it is necessary to have a "worst that can happen" scenario discussion with the start-up team (see page 82 of the text)?

_____

_____

_____

_____

_____

_____

_____

Chapter 13 – Managerial Accounting. Successful start-ups depend on teamwork. The program staff and the management accounting staff must constantly reassess start-up assumptions, review actual numbers against the budget, and chart and navigate course changes to ensure success. Using Exhibit #1 answer a few critical questions:

Discussion question: Variable costs: Name three costs on the start-up budget that are variable costs that change in direct proportion to changes in the student count.

Discussion question: Fixed costs: Name three costs that remain constant regardless of changes in the census.

Discussion question: Relevant range: Pick a variable cost in the budget and explain what the relevant range of this cost is (see pg 135 in the text).

Discussion question: Relevant range: Pick a fixed cost in the budget and explain what the relevant range of this cost is. (Example: rent – 65 students)

Discussion question: Why does a true variable cost like food stay constant for every student added?

_____

_____

_____

_____

_____

Discussion question: Why does a true fixed cost like rent decrease on a per student basis as the student count increases (see page 135 in the text)?

_____

_____

_____

_____

_____

Chapter 14 – Financial Management. TRS was an adjacent business opportunity that emerged because of the success of another human service company under the corporate umbrella. One of the problems that was hurting the parent organization was that it had a few large customers that while significant, were becoming less profitable. Some didn't pay for months, some were controlling rates through rate setting, and some were decreasing the utilization of services. These customers were potentially placing the entire company at an unacceptable level of financial risk.

The team perceived that TRS could help to address this growing concern. This help came in three parts:

1. Diversification of revenue. The goal of TRS was to diversify its customer base so it had many profitable customers (the goal was 20 customers for the total census of 65 students). If TRS had a large number of customers, none of which was too dominant, they could reduce the risk that they would have placed "all of their eggs in one basket." This would avoid the doubling effect of the TRS business risk being ON TOP OF a particular customer's funding risk.

2. Portfolio analysis. Even though TRS would have multiple customers, risk would remain because the service it was providing would be very similar to the service its customers provide. There was also risk inherent in the fact that the great majority of funding would come from government sources. The team identified these as risks, but proceeded anyway, in part because its perception was that IDEA legislation is here to stay and that, for the indefinite future, public schools will continue to operate under a mandate to provide a free and appropriate education to students with disabilities.

3. *Concentration of credit risk.* The positive side of a dependence on IDEA and public school revenue is that, when compared with private pay customers, bad debt from government sources of revenue is virtually nonexistent. With revenue diversified, a cash interruption by any single school district would not be fatal to the program.

Discussion question: What are three ways that having one large customer that accounts for a large proportion of TRS revenue would be bad for the company?

_____

_____

_____

_____

_____

_____

_____

Discussion question: In what ways do you think TRS was right to base its very existence on the federal law IDEA? In what ways was it wrong?

_____

_____

_____

_____

_____

_____

_____

Chapter 15 – Budgeting. The start-up budget for TRS offers a "North Star" or touch point that serves as a reference for any changes that might be needed in staffing, wage rates, and unforeseen circumstances, such as unanticipated regulation. Exhibit #2 analyzes the variance between the budget and actual results from operations. As you can see, staff salaries were overspent during the reported period. Is that good or bad? It depends, but without the variance analysis the questions would never be asked. The budget assumptions are a key component of the operating and start-up budgets and should be made explicit.

Discussion question: List three of the largest variances (shown in Exhibit #2) and explain why you think each of them exists.

Discussion question: List at least two budget assumptions that TRS would have to modify if it obtained the new information that it landed a customer that could supply a constant 50 students (bulk sale).

Chapter 16 – Sales, Marketing, and Generating Revenue. A sale is the complete process of prospecting a customer, closing the transaction, and ultimately delivering cash to the company. At least initially, the chief sales person for TRS was the director, and champion of the program, who was tasked with selling the program to public school districts and to the private pay market. The team believed that a professional sales person was not going to achieve the initial sales results needed to get to breakeven because they would not have a sufficient understanding of, and passion for, the program. TRS elected program knowledge over sales experience and polish. TRS also expected to generate information from its sales contacts and marketing activities that could feed back into operations and result in a better program, more attuned to the needs and concerns of its customers.

Marketing is the science of driving sales by matching the needs of a customer with the skills of the organization. In the case of TRS, the skills of the organization revolved around: (1) managing the behaviors of its students with developmental disabilities, and (2) achieving superior academic progress, when compared to the traditional public school. The team hypothesized that this one-two punch would deliver a significant number of students to its doors.

Marketing strategy is the long-term "plan of action" that drives us towards our revenue goals. TRS strategies included: (1) targeting directors of special education services in public school districts within a 45-minute drive of its site; (2) reaching parents of students with special needs children who were dissatisfied with their current education experience, using the "jungle drum," word of mouth, and other methods; (3) using social media to share successes and to develop a sense of family and community; and (4) focusing on children who are outliers because their various behaviors and social deficiencies make them a challenge to teach in the traditional public school setting.

Discussion question: What are the pros and cons of using a professional sales person versus a human services professional in the sales capacity in this case?

_____

_____

_____

_____

_____

Discussion question: Why do you think the TRS marketing strategy didn't include targeting private schools, charter schools, or voucher programs? Should it have?

_____

_____

_____

_____

_____

Chapter 17 – Pricing. The major challenge of creating the TRS pricing model was that no comparable service offering existed. Although there were a few alternative schools offering non-traditional settings, some operated only a half day, some had weak academic offerings, and still others focused on behaviors only. TRS picked an aggressive daily rate fully aware that it would raise some eyebrows among educators. But the combination of daily rate and normalized number of units of service needed to be high enough to cover not only TRS expenses, but also the administrative overhead of the corporate function and the needed profit. The TRS daily rate is significantly higher than that of most of its apparent competition (in the eyes of the school districts); see Table 1: Daily Rate Comparisons.

Company	Daily Rate
A	$138
B	$150
C	$168
D	$198
TRS	$265

Table 1: Daily Rate Comparisons

The team believed that pricing power was strong due to the fact that (1) few alternatives or substitutes existed and (2) its education services were sorely needed by public school districts that are accountable to state and federal education officials for specific outcomes. These factors supported a relatively "inelastic" pricing model.

Unit pricing has two effects: the price effect and the units-of-service effect. Table 2: Total Revenue Projection shows the effect unit rate was projected to have on total revenue.

Service/Expense	Daily Rate	Projected Yearly School Days Provided at TR	Total Revenue (Dollars)
Company A	$138	10,800*	$1,490,400
Company B	$150	10,800	$1,620,000
Company C	$168	10,800	$1,814,400
Company D	$198	10,800	$2,138,400
TRS – Actual Rate	$265	10,400	$2,756,000
TRS – Proposed	$300	8,800	$2,640,000
TRS – Proposed	$325	7,100	$2,307,500

*180 days @ 60-student capacity

Table 2: Total Revenue Projection

Discussion question: Does the highest price bring in the most revenue? If not, why not?

_____

_____

_____

_____

Discussion question: What is the project census for each rate?

_____

_____

_____

Discussion question: What would happen to the price TRS could charge if the pricing model was more elastic?

_____

_____

_____

_____

Chapter 23 – Real Estate. For TRS to be successful management believed that it needed to operate in a setting that looked and felt like a traditional school. This would help support the widespread belief (and sometime parental dream) that no child with a disability should be excluded from the educational experiences that "normal children" have access to. This was also an objective of IDEA legislation. The typical human services program that is location-based will show 20–25% of its operating costs to be associated with its building. These will include costs like rent, mortgage interest, property taxes, and utilities. There will also be some unusual costs to consider. A common saying in the real estate industry is that the most important factor in choosing a property is "location, location, location." For instance, if you identify a school building that has a perfect layout for your needs, but is 30 miles too far from your target market, you will lose business and may cause higher expenses for those customers you still attract, such as transportation costs. Real estate searches must also be concerned about landing on sites that are too large, too old, too far off a public bus line, or in a community that does not reflect the image and brand you intend to represent.

The TRS team looked at more than 10 school buildings in the Milwaukee area in 2010. The four possibilities that made the final cut were:

1. City of Greenfield – 84th Street School. Vintage 1980, this former elementary school had been closed by the school district as a result of enrollment decline. It needed $500,000 in improvements. It was for sale or lease and was situated less than 10 miles away from the ideal location on the far southwest side of the Milwaukee Metro area. Its capacity was about 100 students. The urban brand of TRS would have been a bit difficult to achieve in this suburban location.

2. City of Greenfield – 51st and Morgan. This school was situated in the perfect location. It was a very attractive functioning public grade school with a capacity of 160 children (80 on each floor). The idea was to split the school in two (first floor, second floor), and to share the common space of the gymnasium, offices, health room, and cafeteria. TRS would occupy the first floor with its special needs population and Greenfield Public Schools would continue to use the second floor for the mainstream student population. A lease-only option, the space had the important caveat that TRS could be "bumped" if rising enrollment meant that GPS needed the extra capacity on the first floor. Grounds were spacious, well-equipped with playground equipment, and adjacent to a municipal park.

3. Vacant parochial school on 42nd and Scott. This setting was functionally sound but needed a facelift to bring it into alignment with the TRS brand identity. This site had the additional advantage of including a convent that would allow TRS to explore the special needs room and board market and the week-on, weekend-off market. However, TRS would have to share the space with a tenant that conducted business unrelated to children's programming. Capacity was 50–55 students. Outside space was limited. It was a lease only with very reasonable rent ($4.50/sq ft) and reasonable terms other than the space sharing feature.

4. Vacant parochial school on 67th and Rodgers. This site was located in a quiet residential area in an adjacent suburb of Milwaukee, the city of West Allis. It was located within four miles of ground zero but slightly off the major community thoroughfares. The school had a capacity of 65 children and had been closed for five years due to declining enrollment. The infrastructure was sound; the gym and cafeteria were air-conditioned, but the classrooms were not. The lease rates were reasonable but no purchase option was available. The parish would consider a right of first refusal. Outside space was limited but extra space was available across the street. The school required $200,000 of leasehold improvements. It had no accessible bathrooms, but had a convent that could eventually be available for eight room and board students (an adjacent business). An eventual purchase was likely.

Discussion question: What are the pros and cons of each site?

Discussion question: Which one would you pick for the first TRS location?

Discussion question: Would you lease or purchase a school location for the first TRS program?

ORP

TRS EXHIBIT #1

EXHIBIT #1

	Year 1				Year 2				Year 3				Year 4			
	BQ1	BQ2	BQ3	BQ4	BQ1	BQ2	BQ3	BQ4	BQ1	BQ2	BQ3	BQ4	BQ1	BQ2	BQ3	BQ4
Revenue																
Fees	17,490	77,910	44,520	161,385	218,493	225,138	160,016	425,141	775,501	666,573	382,240	871,872	783,256	673,239	386,062	880,591
Total Revenue	17,490	77,910	44,520	161,385	218,493	225,138	160,016	425,141	775,501	666,573	382,240	871,872	783,256	673,239	386,062	880,591
Salaries & Benefits																
Salaries and Wages	110,426	148,515	148,515	157,263	131,079	131,080	140,252	156,360	299,115	307,735	311,048	311,048	301,358	310,045	313,382	313,382
Payroll Taxes & Benefits	15,577	19,659	19,659	20,925	22,376	22,371	23,944	26,684	54,978	51,512	51,946	49,315	55,390	51,898	52,336	49,685
Total Salaries & Benefits	126,003	168,174	168,174	178,188	153,455	153,451	164,196	183,044	354,093	359,247	362,994	360,363	356,749	361,943	365,717	363,067
General Expenses																
Staff Training, Recruitment, Benefits	3,600	1,000	600	4,099	2,928	2,928	2,928	2,928	4,746	4,746	4,746	4,762	4,782	4,782	4,782	4,798
Insurance	2,789	2,949	2,949	2,949	2,490	2,490	2,490	2,490	2,826	2,826	2,826	2,826	2,847	2,847	2,847	2,847
Depreciation	2,382	3,573	3,573	3,573	17,301	17,301	17,301	17,301	17,703	17,703	17,703	17,703	17,836	17,836	17,836	17,836
Food & Household Supplies	9,625	10,875	11,875	10,875	6,375	6,375	6,375	6,375	17,286	13,683	12,026	16,176	17,416	13,786	12,116	16,297
Building Rent, Utilities, & R.E. Taxes	26,240	37,860	37,860	37,860	26,607	26,607	26,607	26,607	46,210	43,010	39,610	45,426	46,557	43,333	39,907	45,767
Purchased Services	6,500	9,750	9,750	9,750	11,307	11,307	11,307	11,307	17,339	20,849	11,809	15,126	17,469	21,005	11,898	15,239
Office Supplies & Expenses	54,081	13,497	13,497	13,497	20,448	14,448	14,448	14,448	14,396	12,396	12,396	16,538	14,504	12,489	12,489	16,662
License & Fees	-	-	-	-	-	-	-	-	1,749	1,749	1,749	1,753	1,762	1,762	1,762	1,766
Program Expenses	12,634	3,651	6,651	3,651	7,224	7,224	7,224	7,224	17,716	11,716	7,716	7,752	17,849	11,804	7,774	7,810
Mileage	3,666	2,499	2,499	2,499	1,749	1,749	1,749	1,749	1,248	1,248	1,248	1,256	1,257	1,257	1,257	1,265
Vehicle Gas & Repairs	3,668	5,502	5,502	5,502	2,775	2,775	2,775	2,775	1,575	1,575	1,575	1,575	1,587	1,587	1,587	1,587
Vehicle Leases	4,653	4,653	4,653	4,653	5,331	5,331	5,331	5,331	5,343	5,343	5,343	5,343	5,383	5,383	5,383	5,383
Travel & Lodging	1,200	5,001	5,001	5,001	1,251	1,251	1,251	1,251	375	375	375	375	378	378	378	378
Equipment Expense	1,834	14,251	20,751	20,751	12,471	12,471	12,471	12,471	16,221	16,221	16,221	16,225	16,343	16,343	16,343	16,347
Miscellaneous Non Allowable	-	-	-	-	96	96	96	96	105	105	105	110	106	106	106	111
Financing Fee Expense	-	-	-	-	-	-	-	-	-	-	-	-	-	-	-	-
Management Fee - ODTC	7,095	7,095	7,095	7,095	7,182	7,182	7,182	7,182	8,957	9,134	9,866	9,196	9,024	9,203	9,940	9,265
Management Fee - ORP Mgt	6,735	6,735	6,735	6,735	22,545	22,545	22,545	22,545	65,065	52,621	29,733	62,333	65,553	53,016	29,956	62,800
Total General Expenses	146,702	128,891	138,991	138,490	148,080	142,080	142,080	142,080	238,860	215,300	175,047	224,475	240,651	216,915	176,360	226,159
Total Expenses	272,705	297,065	307,165	316,678	301,535	295,531	306,276	325,124	592,953	574,547	538,041	584,838	597,400	578,858	542,077	589,225
Contribution Margin	(248,480)	(212,420)	(255,910)	(148,558)	(60,401)	(47,752)	(123,619)	122,658	247,718	144,752	(125,963)	349,477	251,515	147,502	(125,953)	354,277
Cumulative Margin	(248,480)	(460,900)	(716,810)	(865,368)	(925,769)	(973,521)	(1,097,140)	(974,482)	(726,764)	(582,012)	(707,975)	(358,498)	(106,983)	40,519	(85,454)	268,842

Exhibit 1

TRS EXHIBIT #2

EXHIBIT #2

	Actual Dec-12	Budget Dec-12	Variance
Revenue			
Fees	1,517,831	1,028,788	489,043
Total Revenue	**1,517,831**	**1,028,788**	**489,043**
Salaries & Benefits			
Salaries and Wages	765,217	558,771	(206,446)
Payroll Taxes & Benefits	119,508	95,375	(24,133)
Total Salaries & Benefits	**884,725**	**654,146**	**(230,579)**
General Expenses			
Staff Training, Recruitment, Benefits	12,072	11,712	(360)
Insurance	10,059	9,960	(99)
Depreciation	70,824	69,204	(1,620)
Food & Household Supplies	45,226	25,500	(19,726)
Building Rent, Utilities, & R.E. Taxes	97,687	106,428	8,741
Purchased Services	55,471	45,228	(10,243)
Office Supplies & Expenses	50,433	63,792	13,359
License & Fees	2,876	-	(2,876)
Program Expenses	38,010	28,896	(9,114)
Mileage	9,003	6,996	(2,007)
Vehicle Gas & Repairs	6,367	11,100	4,733
Vehicle Leases	22,240	21,324	(916)
Travel & Lodging	897	5,004	4,107
Equipment Expense	58,380	49,884	(8,496)
Miscellaneous Non Allowable	500	-	(500)
Financing Fee Expense	599	384	(215)
Management Fee - ODTC	30,484	28,728	(1,756)
Management Fee - ORP Mgt	89,139	90,180	1,041
Total General Expenses	**600,267**	**574,320**	**(25,947)**
Total Expenses	**1,484,992**	**1,228,466**	**(256,526)**
	-	-	-
Contribution Margin	**122,577**	**(109,114)**	**231,691**

Exhibit 2

NOTES

ROYAL ACADEMY

Case Overview

Royal Academy was a human services company created to provide residential treatment services to children and adolescents who entered the United States via the Mariel boatlift mass emigration from Cuba between April 15 and October 31, 1980.

The origins of the boatlift went all the way back to the Cuban revolution in 1959 when Fidel Castro overthrew the Batista government. At that time, hundreds of thousands of Cubans fled by boat to the United States and settled primarily in Miami. Once the revolution had a firm grip on Cuba, the mass exodus of Cubans coming to the United States stopped. This left many Cubans in a state of limbo. Families split, economic conditions deteriorated, and political freedom disappeared literally overnight.

In 1965, a similar boat exodus began, but many lives were lost in the Straits of Florida. The Castro regime then agreed to the U.S. Freedom Flights program, which transported 250,000 Cubans to the United States over the next eight years. To the disappointment of many Cuban Americans, the Castro regime unilaterally ended the flights in 1973.

By 1976, with the election of President Carter, relations with Cuba started to thaw. The Carter administration established an "interest section" in Havana, and the Castro regime did the same in Washington D.C. Small numbers of political prisoners were released to the United States, and some Cuban Americans were allowed to visit relatives on the Cuban mainland. Initially the Carter administration displayed an open policy towards Cuban immigration, and immigrants were granted refugee status. This view changed as it became clear that the Castro government was unloading many of its "undesirables" on the United States, such as criminals, political prisoners, and the mentally ill.

In 1979, a bus carrying several people crashed through the gates of the Peruvian embassy, and the passengers sought political asylum. This was the first of many instances of embassy takeovers by those seeking to leave the island. By April 1980, up to 10,000 people huddled in the Peruvian embassy grounds seeking asylum. The U.S. government responded by invoking the emergency provisions of the Refugee Act of 1980, which provided permission and funding to receive thousands of refugees from the Peruvian embassy on U.S. soil.

Apparently, this was the last straw in a mounting series of embarrassments for the Castro regime. On April 20, 1980, the government announced that all Cubans who wished to flee to the United States were free to board boats at the port of Mariel, Cuba. Within 24 hours after the news broke in Miami, flotillas of pleasure boats were en route to board waiting relatives and others in the Mariel harbor.

Refugees encountered officials from an "alphabet soup" of U.S. agencies when they landed in Key West. Agencies represented included Federal Emergency Management Agency (FEMA), Immigration and Naturalization Service (INS), Border Patrol, Customs, the Coast Guard; the Departments of Defense, State, Justice, and Labor; the General Services Administration; and Health and Human Services. As it turned out, the Cuban government had gathered individuals with criminal backgrounds, mental health issues, physical deformities, and others representing "economic overhead' with groups of everyday refugees for the trip to the United States. These individuals were segregated from the refugee population at large for processing later.

Approximately 125,000 refugees arrived on the shores of the United States between April 15 and October 31, 1980. From among those, the "undesirables" numbered from 7,500 to as high as 40,000. A 1991 Congressional report pegs the number at 31,000.

The "undesirables" and those who had no sponsors or family in the United States were processed and sent to temporary refugee camps, and later to military bases in Pennsylvania, Wisconsin, and Arkansas. Living conditions were tough in these camps. Riots and escapes at Fort Chaffee, Arkansas, became a campaign issue in the re-election defeat of then Governor Bill Clinton.

Royal Academy

By fall 1980, Camp McCoy in Wisconsin still housed about 150 Cuban refugee adolescents who could not be released into society. At that time, Camp McCoy was a seasonal facility, and those individuals had to be vacated by the winter. The INS was in communication with the State of Wisconsin Department of Human Services, which in turn contacted the children's services community to see if any providers could assist in resolving this humanitarian crisis by offering programming and transition services to the adolescents who remained at Camp McCoy.

In early August 1980, a request for proposal (RFP) was issued. The program had to open within 60 days of the RFP date, which would have been October 1, 1980. Responders were in crisis mode, as winter was fast approaching.

In this case study, we will analyze the opening, operation, and closing of Royal Academy as a 44-bed child caring institution (CCI). We will discuss the major reasoning and decision points, following the general outline of *The Business of Human Services*.

Analysis By Chapter

Chapter 3 – Public Policy. It is critical that leaders of a human services company understand and track the major public policy issues that affect its business. Human services differs from many industries in that it cannot be separated from the decisions made by our political leaders. In this case, President Carter, and to some extent Fidel Castro, created the opportunity for Royal Academy. The Refugee Act of 1980 laid the groundwork for the opportunity, and the market for serving this adolescent population was created through the political will of President Carter. Whatever the issue, someone in the company should be assigned to scan the public policy world on a continual basis, scouting for events that represent risk or, in this case, opportunity. The refugee crisis was in the national news each day, and it was impossible to miss. More often, risk or opportunity lurks in the fine print of some bill or policy report. Either way, human services business goes to those who are primed to seek out opportunities and act quickly.

Discussion question: Can you think of another public policy crisis that created the opportunity for the development of a new human services business?

_____

_____

_____

_____

_____

Discussion question: Did you or your company seize the moment and take advantage of the business opportunity? Why or why not?

_____

_____

_____

_____

_____

Chapter 4 – Agency Mission. Though the corporate mission was not clearly defined in 1980, at the time they were serving adolescents in a variety of residential settings who had developmental disabilities or mental illness, or who were high-functioning children caught in the corrections system, often with personality disorders. On the adult side, they were serving both developmentally disabled (DD) and mentally ill (MI) individuals in assorted settings, but were not focusing on community-based services for populations from correction or with a sexual perpetrator background. From the available material gathered at the time, the Cuban adolescent refugee population included individuals who were criminals, mentally ill, or sexual perpetrators, with most being high functioning. Royal Academy considered the main barrier to treatment to be language, as none of the population spoke English.

Discussion question: In what ways do you think this proposed residential program violated its corporate mission?

_____

_____

_____

_____

_____

Discussion question: Do you think the language barrier was too great of a challenge, given the condensed nature of the RFP?

Chapter 5 – Types of Business Entities. Royal Academy was set up as a private, closely held, for-profit corporation. It was part of a controlled group of human services companies. This became an advantage when they needed to act quickly. Royal Academy staff was able to secure and share resources like equipment, start-up staff, operating expertise, and back office business functions that enabled it to open the program within the 60-day window required for the RFP. All related party services were charged at arms-length rates to ensure that liabilities would be separated for this high risk population. Certain corporate attributes were important for operations:

  1. Legal entity/limited liability. A separate legal entity was needed to minimize the risk presented by the new business to the group's other corporations, including risks of contracting, expense reports, and profit calculations.

  2. Centralized management. To run properly, the operation required a separate board of directors, officers, and on-site management segregated by function.

Discussion question: What attributes of corporations made incorporating a desirable choice for this project?

Chapter 6 – Organizational Structure. Royal Academy was a 44-bed residential treatment program located in an urban area in Milwaukee, Wisconsin. It was four miles away from the nearest dependable backup support system, another (CCI) operated by a sister company. The site was segregated by population. Some other human services organizations that received contracts to care and provide programming for the remaining 150 children at Camp McCoy integrated these clients into existing programs and client types. They did not believe this would work for its clients, because to do so would severely disrupt existing programs and client populations. The only integration that occurred was for staffing needs. They used their most seasoned and experienced staff to open the program as quickly as possible, and they shared resources to the extent possible. An on-site director was the point person for the coordination and control of all staff. Departments were set up by function, all reporting to the on-site director except for special corporate expertise, which was provided as needed by the staff of the parent management company.

Discussion question: Do you think it was the right decision to segregate the program at one site, or should they have integrated the refugees into the organization's existing CCI programs that had excess capacity?

Discussion question: Do you think it would have been more cost effective to operate in a segregated setting or in an integrated setting within existing programs?

Chapter 7 – Corporate Culture and Exceptional Leadership. The ultimate goal in any organization is that all players "pull the rope in the same direction." This was tough to accomplish at Royal Academy and was an important factor in leading to the decision to close the program after six months. Although they relied on the best staff from assorted programs, some forces were working against them:

1. The professional human service staff. Some of the children were actually adults, some were mentally ill, some were released from jail, and some were just kids closer to ordinary that had no U.S. sponsor. Most of the residents did not speak English; this communication breakdown made it very difficult to maintain and control the program. In addition, the human services staff became frustrated when executing plans of care. Staff was simply unprepared for what they saw and exasperated at the lack of progress in achieving program goals.

2. Hispanic staff. Bilingual staff were employed who were not human services professionals by trade. The human services professionals, working through bilingual staff, attempted to execute the plans of care with only marginal success. This created triangles of dysfunctions—the client, the human services staff, and the interpreter—that impeded the execution of the plans of care.

3. Cultural differences. The cultural differences between the residents and the staff were striking. In addition to the criminal backgrounds or mental health issues presented by the clients, they came from a country characterized by political persecution, scarcity of food, social unrest, and no respect for authority.

4. Program controls. Each resident was assigned an INS case manager in Miami. These case managers, at times, would second-guess program protocols, making it difficult to meet program expectations. To make matters worse, the Milwaukee Police Department started to ignore crisis calls from program staff when backup was needed. They would also fail to respond to community incidents that involved the residents. Their perception was that the police department believed it had had no authority over these non-citizens, housed in the city under a federal INS contract, and concluded it was fruitless to intervene.

For these and other reasons, the staff of Royal Academy quickly burnt out. Pay was not the issue—wages were well above market—but the work environment became very difficult to manage.

Discussion question: How would you have addressed the corporate culture at Royal Academy?

Discussion question: Do you think paying higher wages would have helped stabilize the program? Why or why not?

_____

_____

_____

_____

_____

_____

Chapter 8 – Licensing and Rule-Making Authority. To be awarded an RFP, secure a location, achieve occupancy, and win a license to operate from a governing authority in less than two months is extremely rare. This demonstrated to them that the Cuban refugee crisis was serious, and all governing agencies with any jurisdiction (federal, state, and municipal) had placed all hands on deck. It is not recalled if the certificate of need provisions were in place to control the issuance of CCI licenses (it is believed they were), but the need was obvious (and probably waived) so that did not hold up the process and shaved months off the typical licensing timeline.

As an organization already operating three CCIs, Royal Academy enjoyed strong relationships with the state licensing authorities and licensing agents in the field. Although the state was desperate to find CCI providers and might have decided to be a bit more lenient with their licensing requirements, Royal Academy was the only agency proposing to open an additional site with a separate 44-bed license. The few other operators who offered services were proposing to do so either in existing facilities, requiring only a population change, or by adding beds to an existing license. They concluded that the licensing authorities could interpret licensing requirements loosely if it was to their advantage or to the advantage of other key government decisionmakers, such as the governor or even the president of the United States.

Discussion question: Do you know of other examples where government authorities exhibited an "all hands on deck" approach to a public policy crisis?

_____

_____

_____

_____

_____

_____

Chapter 9 – Opening a New Program. The refugee crisis, the opening, the life, and the closing of the program all transpired within period of just over a year. The Mariel boatlift began April 20, 1980. Royal Academy opened in early October 1980, and closed by May 31, 1981. It was expected to last three or four years, and it could have led to various other programming opportunities had things gone well. The opening had some unique characteristics:

1. The value proposition. To be successful in operating a human services program, there must be a strong answer to the question: "Why would a customer want to purchase our services?" The answer was because of expected superior performance, customization, and proposed outcomes. The proposed revenue of the program less the expected expenses pointed to a sizable operating margin if events went according to plan (which, at least financially, they did).

2. Clearing bureaucratic hurdles. This is usually one of the most time-consuming, confusing, and frustrating aspects of opening a new program. In this case, the bureaucratic hurdles (federal, state, municipal, internal agency, and staff buy-in) were overcome with great speed and seamless teamwork—something rarely seen in practice.

3. Start-up losses. Royal Academy offered the best possible scenario for a human services program to achieve breakeven rapidly—a very favorable answer to the "time is money" conundrum. All powers lined up to support opening as quickly as possible. Forty-four clients were admitted from Camp McCoy within one week, and the rate provided an acceptable operating margin, with revenue coming from the same state departments that paid for many of the other programs. (On a side note, the State of Wisconsin received reimbursement from INS through a special line item allocation made available under the emergency provisions of the Federal Refugee Act of 1980.)

4. Start-up tasks. A team of current employees diligently worked on all of the start-up tasks, in addition to their "day jobs." They had been selected for their functional expertise, ability to work independently, and demonstration of successful results, all while operating in crisis mode. The planning included (1) finding, securing, and preparing the program site; (2) assessing and screening clients, and completing the paperwork (crisis or no crisis, the customer was still the INS); (3) hiring human services professionals and bilingual staff, and providing staff training; (4) securing the license and necessary zoning permits; and (5) effectively communicating the status of our efforts with all stakeholders during the process.

5. Program location. They got lucky and found a location quickly. It was not the optimal location, but it was settled on because of time pressure. The building was suitable, though the layout called for an inefficient but ultimately acceptable staffing pattern (given the daily rate). Its main problem was that it was located in a densely populated area on a high-traffic thoroughfare that could pose some danger for residents. Fortunately, it was a multiple-use building and proved relatively easy to transfer upon closing the program.

Discussion question: Do you think the value proposition was a sufficient answer to the problem faced by the customer (INS)? Why or why not?

_____

_____

_____

_____

_____

_____

Discussion question: Construct a start-up graph for Royal Academy, paying particular attention to the timing and the slope of the revenue line. Why was this a good scenario for the company (see Graph 9-2 on page 75 in the text)?

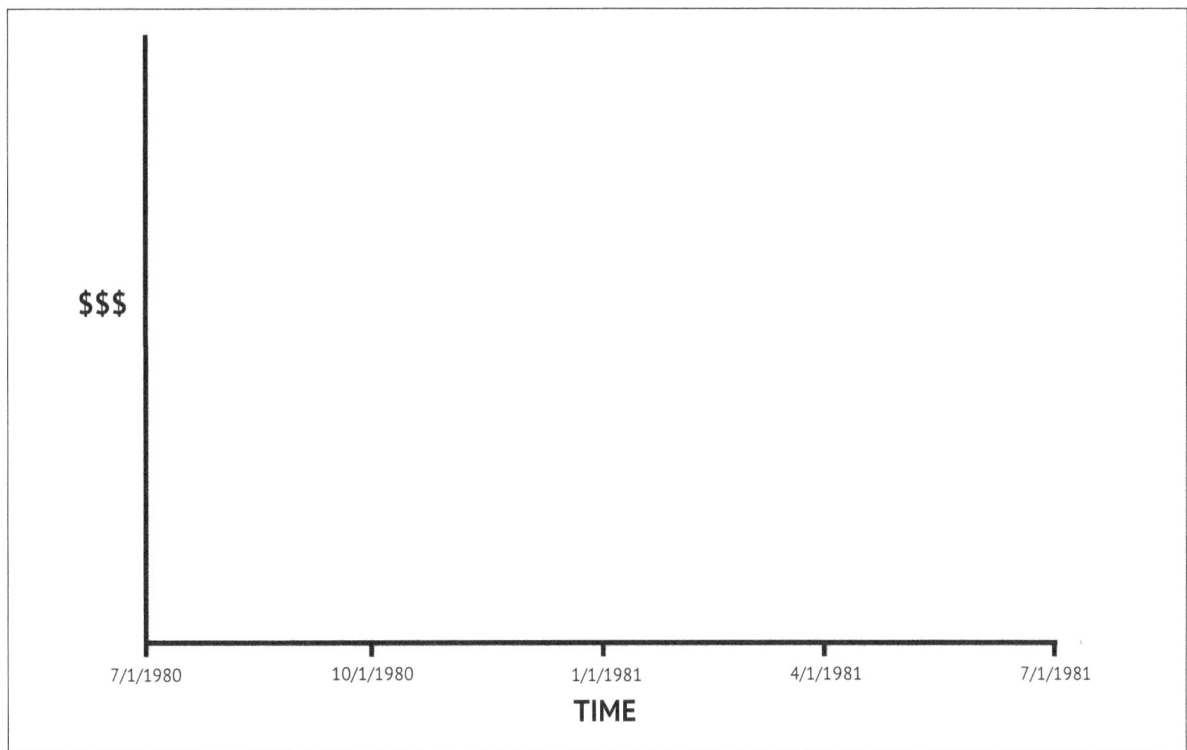

$$\$\$\$$$

7/1/1980   10/1/1980   1/1/1981   4/1/1981   7/1/1981

TIME

_____

_____

_____

Chapter 11 – Closing a Program. Closing a program generally occurs because of money. That was not true in this case. Royal Academy quickly became "financially normalized" but never became "operationally normalized." It soon became apparent that four barriers would prevent it from carrying out the mission over the proposed three-year plus lifespan of the program.

1. Age of residents. The first problem was that they were told the residents would consist of children between the ages of 10 and 17 years. But the clients did not arrive in the United States with any official records from Cuba such as birth certificates or immigration papers. It turned out that at least one-third of the 44 residents were adults in their twenties. U.S. immigration papers contained inaccurate information as a result of language barriers or intentional misrepresentation. This created a dilemma. First, they were plainly licensed as a CCI for children aged 6–17. Second, the zoning permit stated that the operation was to be licensed by the State of Wisconsin, and the permit would expire should that license cease to exist.

2. The police. Each resident had an INS case manager who oversaw the resident's activities. It soon became apparent that the Milwaukee police officials who had contact with the residents were in a predicament because the residents were neither U.S. citizens nor possibly children. INS case managers were difficult for the police to deal with in response to incidents. Over time, the response times lengthened (especially close to shift change), and responses eventually ceased altogether. The writing was on the wall: Royal Academy was on its own.

3. Staff burnout. Most of the human services staff came from existing programs and were drawn to the opportunity because of higher pay, the challenge, and the desire to have a positive impact on the less fortunate. It soon became apparent that the unique mix of mental health, corrections, violence, child, adult, political, cultural, and language barriers would exact its toll on the staff. Most of the staff still show the lasting effects of this episode in their careers.

4. Lack of success in achieving outcomes. This was a strange situation in that the customer seemed quite satisfied with the program as it unfolded, but the effect on the staff was quite the opposite—even a direct negative correlation. The INS seemed content that the residents were off the street and receiving reasonable care, though outcomes were marginal at best. Royal Academy staff looked at the situation differently. They feared serious injury—or worse—to staff, other residents, or to neighbors. They began to see that positive outcomes were very unlikely. Sooner or later, luck was going to run out, and they became concerned about the potential effects of a major incident on other operations. Perhaps a permanent settlement at Camp McCoy had not been a bad idea after all.

The INS was notified around the end of March 1981 that Royal Academy was closing. They began discharge planning for the residents and closed in May 1981. The INS was not happy with the decision to close the program before the three years were over. The task of processing 125,000 Cubans for life in the United States was still in a critical phase. Eventually, fewer than 4,000 were returned to Cuba because they were unacceptable for political asylum, while the rest remained in the United States.

INS stopped returning calls trying to coordinate discharge planning. Not getting any response, Royal Academy staff delivered the remaining 25 residents to the INS office on a Friday afternoon late in May and closed up shop. It was later learned that these residents moved into temporary housing at the Milwaukee Downtown YMCA and then dispersed into American society.

Discussion question: Create a closure graph of the Royal Academy program. Pay particular attention to the slope of the revenue line. Explain its effects on the closure loss (see Graph 11-1 on page 101 in the text).

$$\text{\$\$\$}$$

| 7/1/1980 | 10/1/1980 | 1/1/1981 | 4/1/1981 | 7/1/1981 |

TIME

Discussion question: Do you think the decision to close Royal Academy prematurely made sense? What are your arguments for or against the closure?

_____

_____

_____

_____

_____

_____

Chapter 15, 17, and 18 – Budgeting, Pricing, and Rate Regulation. Given the two-week time frame for submitting the response to the RFP, they had access to very limited information before submitting their proposal to the INS via the State of Wisconsin. They submitted the response before they had secured a site location (so occupancy costs were impossible to project) and before they had screened the clients (making staffing patterns hard to predict), which thereby raised the financial risk that costs would be overloaded. Royal Academy had pricing power because few substitutes existed; they had the operating expertise; and the services were vital, necessary, and needed immediately. They were subject to Wisconsin Allowable Costs for the contract because it was being administered by the state for INS. This meant that they were free to set their own rates, but profit would be capped at 7.5% of allowable expenses with no chance of earning the extra 2.5% on expenses from the equity calculation (for a total of 10% on allowable expenses) because, as a new operation without previous earnings, Royal Academy would have no equity. It also did not have time to think about the pricing problem for very long.

With those constraints, it developed the following pricing strategy. They compared the new program to a 50-bed residential treatment program for DD adults in the Milwaukee area that they operated at the time. They made the following adjustments to the operating budget:

1. They doubled the direct care staffing pattern because they needed to pair human service professionals with smart (large) Spanish-speaking men who could help bridge the language barrier, help control the premises, and help to bridge the perceived cultural gaps.

2. They paid 20–30% above market for all positions to help ensure a lower turnover and enhance quality.

3. They paid signing bonuses for those who started immediately to defray the costs of leaving current jobs.

4. They changed the divisor on the base budget from 50 to 44, using the costs for the 50-bed program in the rate calculation for the 44-bed program.

5. They added a risk factor to the budget, knowing that if they generated excess profit, they would be able to refund it to the State of Wisconsin when they submitted the compliance reports at the end of the year.

This gave them an adjusted rate that was about 80% higher than the budget and rate borrowed from the 50-bed program. They estimated the proposal's chance of being accepted was high, given the conditions on the ground. They protected themselves financially as much as possible, considering they had to respond without conducting typical due diligence.

Discussion question: Do you think the rate setting strategy was sound? If not, what would you have done differently?

Chapter 24 – Insurance. Risk occurs when an individual or organization is exposed to the chance that something bad will happen. Human services organizations require various types of insurance to protect the interests of the shareholders or not-for-profit organizations so the corporate mission can be pursued without interruption. In this case, they became concerned that, as an agency and perhaps even personally, they could be held liable for the harm residents caused to others or themselves. After operating the first few months, they grew concerned that they had a "tiger by the tail." The risk of unintentional injury to other persons or damage to their property through negligence or carelessness was becoming a problem that required attention. This risk seemed different from any they had encountered in other settings. Given the constraints placed on them by the INS and licensing authorities, they were concerned the police could not protect employees, the neighborhood, or other residents from very serious events that were thought likely to occur—and the Royal Academy staff could not protect them, either. Despite the best intentions of management, the company could be held responsible for actions or inactions committed by an employee or its residents. In that event, no excuse could shift the blame to the state or INS, and no insurance could protect the company from potentially significant financial repercussions. And, of course, no insurance protects an agency's reputation.

Discussion question: How would you handle the potential risks of serving this population?

Discussion question: What measures could you put in place to protect the company, other residents, the neighborhood, and the employees?

_____

_____

_____

_____

_____

_____

NOTES

THE STRATEGIC RENEWAL CUSTOMER MATRIX

Background

Sara is the executive director of a human services agency that provides an assortment of services for people with disabilities. It employs over 325 people and serves nearly 200 children and young adults at any one time. Its major services include residential options, educational tutoring services, emergency respite, in-home supports, and diagnostic and evaluation services. Though a non-profit, the agency had generated a surplus for four years that added to its fund balance, now into eight digits. Before then, operations had not generated a surplus for over six years. This caused the fund balance to become alarmingly low and jeopardize the very existence of the business.

The board of directors consisted mostly of individuals who meant well but did not have the time, expertise, or desire to help the agency in its time of need. In fact, most on the board were only interested in the fundraising activities of the organization, which were becoming less and less successful as finances deteriorated. Fortunately, the board did have a few skilled individuals who became actively involved in the turnaround needed to keep the agency afloat.

Eight years ago, when the agency was clearly starting to fail, these individuals took it upon themselves to assess what was wrong, to decide what fixes were necessary, and to implement a plan of correction to nurse the agency back to health. Part of this solution was to replace the executive director with a new hire, Sara, who had explicit instructions to implement a roadmap to get the agency on a better financial footing. These board members knew the truth of the saying "no margin, no mission," and they did not want their organization to become a casualty of that principle.

Analysis

An assessment of the financials showed that although occupancy, direct care costs, and general expenses were at acceptable levels, certain programs did not margin, bad debt was increasing, some services were being provided without reimbursement, and some administrative costs were excessive. An analysis was undertaken under the watchful eye of a board member with the assistance of the accounting firm, the corporate lawyer, the executive director Sara, and the internal corporate controller.

After six months of hard work, working for days on end, the team exposed some problems that required immediate attention if the organization was to return to a position of financial health. The analysis determined that:

1. The daily rates for certain customers had not been adjusted to market, nor had they kept pace with the costs of providing the services.

2. Three customers accounted for most of the bad debt.

3. Certain programs were providing free services or were being manipulated by a savvy customer due to "bed hold days" not being paid for.

4. The administrative office had recently added four staff to "help" with the billing process for one of its largest customers, shifting the customer's overhead to the agency, effectively causing a rate decrease.

The results of the analysis had a common theme: the organization's financial problems grew because it failed to manage its customers. They were winning with some customers and losing with others. The team decided it would do little good to play the victim and blame customers for their predicament; they preferred to become "a player" in the situation by taking responsibility for their role in its creation. The team took a candid inventory, exposed the shortcomings of the organization, and decided to solve the problem by focusing on response-ability.

Relying on the Strategic Renewal Matrix (page 182 of the text), Sara ranked each of its nearly 60 customers according to annual sales dollars. Then she assessed each customer, one by one, by looking at three criteria:

1. *Was the customer strategic (very important to the long-term success of the agency)?*
2. *Was the customer significant (provided substantial revenue or had the potential to do so)?*
3. *Was the customer profitable?*

When she got to the twentieth customer, Sara stopped the exercise because these 20 customers accounted for 96% of total agency revenue. In fact, Sara could cover 60% of the revenue by looking at only five customers.

Results. What Sara discovered was good news and bad news.

- *Customer A (20% of total revenue).* The distinguishing feature of customer A was that although it was strategic and significant, it was only marginally profitable, for two reasons:

  - *Serving the customer required excess administrative staff.* The agency added four full-time employees several years earlier to help reduce accounts receivable "days outstanding" to a more reasonable level of 40 days from the historical 80 days, and to reduce the billing error rate from 8% to 2%.

  - *The customer refused to reimburse the agency for "bed hold days" stemming from frequent hospitalizations of eight of its clients.*

- *Customer B (15% of total revenue).* Fortunately, this customer was strategic, significant, and profitable—exactly the type of high value customer that the agency wanted to attract.

- ***Customer C (10% of total revenue).*** Customer C ranked third because although it had the same percentage of total revenue as customer D, it did so with 50% fewer clients. It was not strategic because it offered little prospect for growth. In fact, the agency had forecasted a revenue decline in each of the next five years. Yet, the customer was significant, and it was profitable.

- ***Customer D (10% of total revenue).*** This customer had the lowest dollars of revenue per client of any of the major customers. It was strategic because of its long-term funding stability, significant due to its significant growth potential, but only marginally profitable because of the extra overhead needed to service the relatively large number of clients. Management also determined that the agency had not pushed to get rate increases because of its belief that it could capture significant increases in volume with the lower rates.

- ***Customer E (5% of total revenue).*** This customer was not strategic, significant, or profitable. In fact, it was the largest producer of bad debt for three years running and frequently won the annual "most difficult customer" award that was strategically placed in the break room at the home office.

Discussion question: What should Sara's goal be with any customer?

Discussion question: What should Sara do with Customer A?

Discussion question: What should Sara do with Customer B?

_____

_____

_____

_____

_____

_____

Discussion question: What should Sara do with Customer C?

_____

_____

_____

_____

_____

_____

Discussion question: What should Sara do with Customer D?

_____

_____

_____

_____

_____

_____

Discussion question: What should Sara do with Customer E?

_____

_____

_____

_____

_____

NOTES

NOTES

INDEX